GOD'S FIRE WALL HEALING OF THE SOUL

SESSION 1 – THE LIGHT

By Robin Kirby-Gatto

© 2013, 2016 by Robin Kirby-Gatto

Table of Contents

Dedication

I would like to first dedicate this series to my husband, Rich Gatto, who has been God's greatest instrument in my healing process, showing me the unconditional love of Christ. Also, I would like to thank my two sons, Christopher and Matthew Kirby, who have been a joy in life and have taught me how to love through the unfailing love of Christ! I want to thank my parents, David and Rebecca Ward, who countlessly poured out unto my soul while I was growing up, conditioning me in a love that was unfailing! I want to thank Sherry Steadham, who is a dear friend that has not only loved me but also been a fashioning instrument for God's Fire Wall Ministry!

A Grateful Heart!

Robin

Forward

Healing of the Soul has impacted my life; God used it to literally HEAL my soul! I have sat underneath Robin in both schools of God's Fire Wall School of the Prophets and Healing of the Soul.

As I sat under these teachings month after month for four years I was left pierced so deeply that there were times when all I could do between sessions, was sit in total silence because the word was colliding with wounded places in my soul and bringing healing because of the revelation of the love of God my soul received!!

As Robin would teach year one about the anatomy of the body in both schools, my typical response was, "WHAT!! OH MY GOSH!!" I realized that God was so much bigger than I ever understood!

After I learned about the heart, ear, lungs and nose I realized, Wow! I truly am beautifully and wonderfully made!!! HUMANITY TRULY IS A MASTERPIECE FROM THE HAND OF GOD, WHICH BLEW MY MIND!!

The same God that I struggled to allow see every place inside of me that was crying out, I got to know through every teaching of Healing of the Soul, because I saw the word of God with new eyes!!! Every teaching has impacted me differently; each one has been used as a step as I climbed my way to TOTAL FREEDOM!

Each time Robin taught on a gate in the Healing of the Soul, I would have a "wow moment." One gate in particular left me literally undone by Gods love!!! The Mercy Gate pierced me so deeply that by the end of the teaching I was on my face crying! I saw Jesus, the Lamb of God in such a fresh way that all I could do was cry; it was like I met him for the very first time!!! I just didn't want to leave that gate and I wanted to stay there!! I MET HIS MERCY ALL OVER AGAIN THAT DAY!!!! It forever changed me!!!

There is so much I could write about; there are so many moments Holy Spirit did surgery on me while Robin was teaching. The mark that these teachings have left on me, are eternal! I only thought I was radically saved before I started Healing of the Soul! Now I'm a RADICAL, TWISTED STUMP THAT GOT HEALED BY THE WORD OF GOD!!!!

Thank you Robin for stepping out so long ago and doing Healing of the Soul!! The seeds that were planted in the ground of this soul right here are growing, growing, and growing!!! Your obedience in writing and teaching has eternal reward!

In the words of an old song, "Thank you for giving to the Lord, I am a life that is changed!" *Sherry Kelly Steadham*

Preface

Where do I even start with this teaching series of God's Fire Wall Healing of the Soul? First I feel honored that God chose me for this work, knowing the power of His love greater through these teachings that have reached out and changed lives. This purview of the complexities of the soul, which is formed and fashioned by God, is going to amaze you.

I share my own process in this series, showing how God healed my soul, bringing deliverance and freedom. Having a background in social work (bachelors and masters), along with a law degree (Juris Doctorate), caused my comprehension of the Word of God in this area to be heightened. As God gave me understanding from what I already knew and then began to reveal His Word, it took me by surprise to see the secret mysteries He had that were fenced in and hidden.

God's Fire Wall Healing of the Soul reveals the display of God's grace, as He opens His Word to show the blueprint of man's soul. The School of Healing of the Soul walks deeply in the book of Nehemiah as we look at Jerusalem to see the revealing of the waste places that were rebuilt by the prophet Nehemiah.

As we step into the book of Nehemiah, you will see it in a way that will leave you in awe, as we journey to each gate, structure, scene, and circumstance, causing you to feel the presence and power of God, as He heals you. Having worked intensely with different mental health diagnosis it has been my firm belief that this component of wisdom is what many are missing in order to be made whole.

Moreover, for the person who simply wants to know the Word of God at such depths, as never before, this series is phenomenal. Once you eat of the Word in the first book you will be enthusiastic, knowing that the Word of Truth is life unto the soul. This book is to be digested in different sittings, and not all at once. Moreover, you will most likely have to read this book again in order to see the mysteries that you might have missed.

God has me teach on a deep level to reveal His mysteries for those who are hungry to walk in the deep places. When a person walks in the deep places of God's Word, it is necessary to let Holy Spirit process the Word in you. That is why I would suggest doing one book a month. You might look at this book and laugh and say "one book a month," thinking you could read all 27 books in a week. However, I would bring attention and say that it is too much meat to eat.

God gave me both God's Fire Wall School of the Prophets and Healing of the Soul to be done alongside each other, providing God's disciple a depth of richness of both the Soul of God (School of the Prophets) and the soul of man (Healing of the Soul). As you journey through both of these schools together I would recommend you do only one book of each, a month and continue to read that book each week for the month.

Once you enter and taste of God's Word and the richness of His love, you will draw closer to God. The fruitfulness of your faith will increase as you journey through these pages.

The scripture that Healing of the Soul is based on is 3 John 1:2.

"2 Beloved, I pray that you may prosper in every way and [that your body] may keep well, even as [I know] your soul keeps well and prospers." 3 John 1:2 Amp

As your soul prospers, you will come to find out that God will prosper you in life and in health. Read simply believing God's Word and knowing the power of His truth!

God bless you!

Robin Kirby-Gatto

Chapter 1 Genesis 1 Let There Be Light!

"7 But as for me, I will look to the Lord and confident in Him I will keep watch; I will wait with hope and expectancy for the God of my salvation; my God will hear me. 8 Rejoice not against me, O my enemy! When I fall, I shall arise; when I sit in darkness, the Lord shall be a light to me." Micah 7:7-8 Amp

The soul, although complex and multifaceted can be seen in God's Word. It is in the secret mysteries, revealed in the Hebrew text of the scripture, which causes the unknown of man's soul to be known, to those who seek knowledge. As Holy Spirit combines scriptures to interpret them from the book of Nehemiah with other books throughout the Old Testament and New Testament, He will bring revelation of truths that will cause better understanding as to why we think and act the way we do.

In December 2011, I engaged Holy Spirit regarding a right now "word" to give out to God's people to offer them hope and encouragement. It was to my surprise that He gave me a download of the soul of man, and the structure that explains how the soul is set. This totally blew me away because I was expecting one revelation, and not an entire plethora of revelations that would leap off of God's Word and show me the soul of man.

Since 2006 God had given me dreams, for which I did not have the interpretation, that were now being revealed to me as it related to my own soul. God flooded me with the interpretation of dreams that had been "on the shelf," so to speak for years, and now opened them up to me in a greater measure than I could have known.

Even after I wrote my first session on Healing of the Soul in December of 2011 for the January 2012 meeting, God confirmed this series. Two days before leaving to teach the first session in Mobile, Alabama I saw a personalized car tag that said "SOULFD," meaning "soul food." God always confirms Himself to me many times through personalized car tags that are exactly what I am about to teach or have already taught. It blew me away that this one was so specific.

In addition, right around the time I began "Healing of the Soul," the Kia Soul was the "big little car" of the time. It was a little car that was a big hit! God kept speaking to me saying that He wanted to bring a book that would be a vehicle to heal man's soul, which is based out of the Word of God. I know for myself, it was God's Word with His Holy Spirit that healed me. God delivered me of so much oppression, casting out demonic strongholds over my soul, by the power of His truth, which is why I am fully persuaded of the Power of His Word.

It was interesting the other day, while I had been editing this first book again in December 2016; I came across another personalized license plate tag that had "JOHN832." I did not know that this scripture was already in this book when I took the picture of the tag; I had not come to that portion of the editing, until two days later. I knew that this was confirmation as to the editing and publication of Healing of the Soul on the Internet for a larger audience; John 8:32 is my testimony and life!

"32 And you will know the Truth, and the Truth will set you free." John 8:32 Amp

God has revealed His truth to me in such large measure that I know it has the power to release you out of your prison(s). It is for this reason that I am so passionate about the WORD OF GOD and the power of it to work in the lives of those who would but hold it dear; it is the power of the Word that sets you free!

As we look at the story of Jesus' birth in Bethlehem we see that the WORD was "wrapped in swaddling clothes" and laid in a manger.

"12 And this will be a sign for you [by which you will recognize Him]: you will find [after searching] a Baby wrapped in swaddling clothes and lying in a manger." Luke 2:12 Amp

The word "swaddle" actually means to wrap in strips or layers of fabric.[i] This word is synonymous with the word "envelop." The word "envelop" means to "wrap up, cover or surround completely." It comes from an Old French word that is composed of "in" and "develop."[ii] Develop signifies a growth and maturity of something.

Therefore, as we look at the swaddling clothes put on Jesus (The Word) at the time of His birth, we get a revelation of the truth of God's Word. As Jesus was "swaddled" at His birth, likewise, we are to cover and surround the Word of God in our heart. It is in our heart, where the Word grows and matures in that place. As the Word of God matures in our soul, then the very thing that is encased in our heart will be made known to us.

BELIEVING BY FAITH!

As I stepped out in faith to do "God's Fire Wall Healing of the Soul," not long after I started "God's Fire Wall School of the Prophets," it blew my mind at the continual downloads (revelations) God would give me.

Each month we would gather to hear the latest teachings and revelations that Holy Spirit would bring, in Birmingham, Alabama. It was very scary at first stepping out each month and hosting a meeting, where I had not written any materials yet, trusting that God would bring me the truth of His Word.

I started the schools as our ministry went to a new level, after we moved to a new address. Rich and I have walked in faith as our ministry would continue to grow and for some reason it was always affirmed each time God would move us to a new address; the address prophesied our season. It all began in 2003 when I asked God three things, which were to take down my idols, give me prudence and humble me, finding that the idol in my heart had been "things," which I owned, including our home. When God delivered me from alcoholism I began decorating everything like crazy, doing wall treatments, redesigning our home and making it uniquely ours. I threw myself into creative work and found myself in time, allowing the house to be my idol.

After God heard my request in exposing the idols of my heart, giving me prudence and humbling me, it was to my discovery that He answered my prayer. We lost that house as well as the vehicle I drove and found ourselves not being able to hold on to anything other than God and each other. It felt as though everything was stripped from me, after asking God to do those three things. However, it was this stripping that became the beginning. God began a process of truly bringing me deeper in His Word. This stripping landed us at a new address on "Warrior Drive."

It was on Warrior Drive where the ministry "Princess Warriors" started and the place in which I wrote "The Glory to Glory Sisterhood" series. Afterward God moved us to a bigger home on "Eagle Drive," where I discovered the "molting process" that an eagle goes through, which I have to say was the hardest time in our lives. Eagle Drive was the place where we started 22 Is 22 (Isaiah 22:22 Company), a prayer ministry providing a safe platform for young people to be able to pray freely.

God then moved us to Pilgrim Lane where Rich was laid off from work. It caused us to lean on God all the more to live like Pilgrims of Faith as those identified in Hebrews 11. It was at Pilgrim Lane, where I went into full-time ministry, and the ministry "God's Fire Wall" came into being. I did not know the purpose for the ministry at the time; I only knew that Zechariah 2:5 "God's Fire Wall" was to be our ministry and out of obedience stepped out into that call. God brought me favor and a lady contacted me to put up a website for the ministry.

It was later when we moved to "Eagle Park Road" on "The Crest," in Eagle Point, where I found out the purpose for our ministry "God's Fire Wall." It would be this ministry whose sole purpose was to equip the body of Christ Jesus as God's Special Forces, knowing the Word in Power, breathing life into them so they could be army of the Living God. The only means by which such a force of people would come together is first of all by truly knowing God and then secondly by being healed.

For twenty-three months I stepped out in faith, having meetings at the house on Eagle Park Rd, not knowing what God would give me for the "School of Healing of the Soul." Not only did we do 23 months of Healing of the Soul at that address, but also 36 months of meetings for "School of the Prophets." It was to my great joy, to find each month would exceed the prior month's teaching. I never thought God could outdo the prior teaching because the revelation was so profound, but He always did.

As I began to write and teach Healing of the Soul, God showed me how it would be so in depth that it would take months for us to get the full understanding through the teachings He provided, about the soul of man. God showed me with this series that it would not be a "fast" or "speedy" thing, but rather a slow process in which we would learn about the soul of man. He revealed to me that as we are made in His image, that it would profane Him to put the entire teaching on man's soul in one book or on a few cds.

Think about that saint; if we are truly made in the image of God then how can we study the soul of man in a few short readings or teachings? God told me that if man was created in His image, the very fact that we reveal God's glory justifies giving time and study to the soul of man designed by God, as revealed in scripture, instead of making it a microwave meal.

A GLIMPSE INTO THE SOUL'S PROCESS

Holy Spirit took me to the book of Nehemiah and showed me the city Jerusalem that had been torn down. In the city are 12 Gates, a wall and other identified structures, which Nehemiah restored. It was in the structures of the city in the book of Nehemiah, that God showed me the Jerusalem of our soul, and its twelve gates and the inner workings of the structures in the city.

He reminded me of the teaching He gave me in 2010, "Awake Awake Oh Sleeper, the Warrior Bride is a Holy City!" It was in that teaching where Holy Spirit began to show me the soul of a person in greater measure, while doing ministry. Continually as I ministered to others, God had me speak to the "Holy City" within them, building others up in His Word by the Spirit of Truth.

The light of God's truth has pierced the soul of many, setting them free and taking them to a greater level of anointing. It is through this process of the soul and how it overcomes darkness, where we will begin to build a foundation of the truth of God's Word.

The word "structure" is both a noun and a verb. The noun part of "structure" means "the arrangement of and relations between the parts or elements of something complex," as well as "a building, and the quality of being organized." The verb form of structure means, "construct or arrange according to a plan," as well as "give a pattern or organization to." The word "structure" comes from the Latin word "struere," meaning "to build."[iii]

As we look at this word closer we will see that this is the perfect word, which God titles the first section of this series "The 12 Gates." In each session (book) on "The 12 Gates" there are 2 main classes (sections), "Structure" and "Revelation." The first part of Healing of the Soul is focused on the Gates of Jerusalem looking intently at Nehemiah chapters one through three. As we look at the "structure" of Jerusalem in Nehemiah 1-3, we will see the structure of our soul and nearly most of the gates. We will finish the last two gates after Nehemiah 3, once we go further throughout the series. Therefore, in this book and the next 12 books for God's Fire Wall Healing of the Soul, we will see two specific sections, "Structure," and "Revelation." As we study one specific truth under the section "Structure," we will then bring in the book of Nehemiah under the section "Revelation," and see the revealing of God's structure in our soul.

Again, the word "structure," is derived from the Latin word "struere" meaning, "to build." That is exactly what God did when He created man; He built (framed) us.

"14 I will confess and praise You for You are fearful and wonderful and for the awful wonder of my birth! Wonderful are Your works, and that my inner self knows right well. 15 MY FRAME WAS NOT HIDDEN FROM YOU WHEN I WAS BEING FORMED IN SECRET [and] intricately and curiously wrought [as if embroidered with various colors] in the depths of the earth [a region of darkness and mystery]. 16 Your eyes saw my unformed substance, and in Your book all the days [of my life] were written before ever they took shape, when as yet there was none of them." Psalm 139:14-16 Amp

The word "frame" in Psalm 139:15 is the Hebrew word `otsem pronounced ō' tsem meaning "power, body, might, strong and substance."[iv] The word "substance" is used in the King James Version for the word "frame." "Frame" comes from the Hebrew root word `atsam pronounced ä tsam' meaning "to bind fast, to close the eyes, to make powerful or numerous, to break the bones, to be great, be increased, be wax, be mightier, be more, shut, become, and make stronger."[v]

The Hebrew word for "bone" is `etsem pronounced eh'tsem meaning "a bone (as strong), by extension, the body, the substance, life, strength, etc."[vi] Thus, the bone indicates the "substance of life," which we will study in greater detail another time; it is in the bone that red blood cells are produced. Therefore, bones represent substance in a person.

When looking at man's anatomy, we see that the skeleton is the framework of man's structure, which is composed of bones. Without the bones there is no means by which muscles can attach, be positioned and rest. The Hebrew word we see here for the word "frame" indicates the "BONES," which is the means by which LIFE IS BUILT! God brought Adam out of dust and in so doing created a structure by which he would be fashioned. After Adam was made and longed for a helpmate, God put Adam asleep and removed his "rib," which is a bone.

"22 And the rib or part of his side which the Lord God had taken from the man He built up and made into a woman, and He brought her to the man." Genesis 2:22 Amp

The Hebrew word for "rib" is *tsela*` pronounced *tsā lä'* meaning "a rib, (figuratively it means) 'a door,' (architecturally) it means 'a floor or ceiling, a timber or plank, beam, board, rib, and side chamber.'"[vii] From the "rib" God did "build" the woman. The word, "build" here in Hebrew from Genesis 2:22 is *banah* pronounced *bä nä'* meaning, "to build, obtain children, builder, repair, set, set up and surely."[viii]

As we look at the rib, not only does it signify a part of the bone structure in Adam, it also represents a "side chamber," which entails the flooring, ceiling and walls of a room. In addition, the "rib" means "a door." Therefore, the rib was a door for the structure of man; it was the door to his lungs, where the essence of life would be contained. The purpose for the ribs are to encase the lungs and it is in the lungs where we have the breath of life and also purification of blood, through the blood gas barrier, which we will do in greater detail in book 9 of God's Fire Wall School of the Prophets.

Looking at the rib alone, we see that there is a relationship between structures of our body where complex actions are carried out between them, allowing us to function at optimal level. If one of those actions in the area of our ribs is not working then its relationship with other parts of our body are seen through what we know as symptoms, allowing doctors to diagnose a disease.

It is no different with our soul! Our soul has a structure that is based on the interworking of an arrangement designed by God, where there are relations among the parts, and those relations are a part of something COMPLEX! The word "complex" means, "consisting of many different and connected parts."[ix] Therefore, like the city Jerusalem having 12 gates and all the different intricacies that composed the city, where one part of the city was not working properly, then other parts of the city were affected. For instance, without the wall being built, the city was not resilient against attacks.

Likewise, in our soul, as the city Jerusalem, it is composed of gates and intricate details that when one thing is injured, it affects our entire person. We see that with the fall of Adam and Eve, where death entered earth and satan was given dominion, a state of spiritual darkness came over the earth. The tree of the knowledge of good and evil manifested a spiritual death, not only affecting man but also the entire world. (See Romans 8:18-23)

Before coming into salvation we had the structure of darkness manifest in our person as a result of the first Adam's fall. It was as though we too, came from that "rib," (chamber of darkness), simply waiting for the light! When we came into salvation in Christ Jesus, the structure of our soul then shifted from the first Adam to the Last Adam!

"Thus it is written, The first man Adam became a living being (an individual personality); the last Adam (Christ) became a life-giving Spirit [restoring the dead to life]." 1 Corinthians 15:45 Amp

Jesus being the last Adam is a "life giving Spirit," representing the Tree of Life in the Garden of Eden. The two trees that are spotlighted in the Garden of Eden are the Tree of Life and the tree of the knowledge of good and evil.

Both of these trees had fruit that would manifest itself in the bodies of Adam and Eve. The Tree of Life has a life sustaining fruit and the tree of the knowledge of good and evil has the manifestation of death. Therefore, as we come into salvation, its as though we have been sitting in that side chamber of darkness in the rib of the first Adam, which represents the world. While sitting in that place of darkness, Christ Jesus comes to pluck us up and bring us into His chamber, the chamber of the Last Adam. Here He brings us into the Light of His presence, giving us a new structure, which is one of life!

We will get into this in more depth throughout the book, but it is necessary to differentiate the truth that when you are brought into salvation you are removed from that old structure of the first Adam. Although we are removed from that structure and brought into the new one in Christ Jesus, our mind still needs to be renewed so that we have the understanding and thinking of our new structure.

It is no different than renovating a house. During a renovation you find wood that is rotted and mold within the walls. If you keep that old structure and put brand new paint over it, that does not change the fact that it is the old structure. However, if you were to renovate a home and kept only that which is good, building on top of it new boards and walls that were fresh, the structure would be sure. Our soul can be compared to the house being renovated. What has to be "new" is that our spirit is born from above! When our spirit is born from above, we still have the same soul, but that soul has to be RENOVATED! The soul is renovated by the transforming power of God's Word in our lives.

THE DREAM!

"7 But as for me, I will look to the Lord and confident in Him I will keep watch; I will wait with hope and expectancy for the God of my salvation; my God will hear me. 8 Rejoice not against me, O my enemy! When I fall, I shall arise; when I sit in darkness, the Lord shall be a light to me." Micah 7:7-8 Amp

This scripture of Micah 7:8 was the first dream God gave me in 2006, revealing my own soul. I did not have understanding at the time to what God was telling me so it was not until late 2011 that God interpreted this dream.

In the dream, I was in the middle of a set of columns all placed in a circle. As I was standing in the middle of them, I saw that my husband, Rich, was standing with me. As I turned in the midst of the columns, I saw the minister of music from our church, whose name is Micah. I looked around at the details of this place, seeing that I was dressed in a white eyelet dress, as I stood there barefoot.

Around my left arm was a scarlet ribbon with a gold bell attached to it. In my right hand was a candleholder with a white candle lit aflame. Outside of the columns was utter darkness. Micah instructed me to go into the darkness, taking the light and to use the bell as I went.

I drew near the edge of the circle close to the columns, and began stepping out into the darkness with the candle while ringing the bell. As I went out into the darkness I was not scared but rather I was strengthened by the bell on my wrist, the light in my hand and the fact that I knew my husband was with me. I had great confidence jingling the bell on my left wrist as I continued to hold the candle.

It was in late 2011 that Holy Spirit showed me what the dream meant. The place in which I was standing was my soul. The columns represented Spiritual Zion, as I was in that "side chamber" (the rib) of the Last Adam, knowing I was born from above and a part of the Spiritual Zion. The root word to Zion in Hebrew actually means "guiding pillar, sign, title and waymark,"[x] which I have always imagined to be like a column or pillar.

"22 But rather, you have come to Mount Zion, even to the city of the living God, the heavenly Jerusalem, and to countless multitudes of angels in festal gathering, 23 And to the church (assembly) of the Firstborn who are registered [as citizens] in heaven, and to the God Who is Judge of all, and to the spirits of the righteous (the redeemed in heaven) who have been made perfect," Hebrews 12:22-23 Amp

Since I am from that Holy City of the Spiritual Zion, in that side chamber of being in Christ Jesus, I was given the Light of God's Truth to take it through the rest of my soul. Areas of my soul had darkness and were in need of the light of Christ Jesus. As I went out with great hope and boldness into the dark places of my soul ringing the bell and shining the light, while my husband came with me, the deeper revealing of what God's Word was doing in my soul was made real! Jesus is my Bridegroom and He comes with me to those dark places of my soul that have not received the Light of Truth. The Word was renovating my soul!

In this place of ringing the bell on my wrist, Holy Spirit showed me the bells at the bottom of the High Priests garments, which jingle while they enter the Holy of Holies once a year. In the Holy of Holies there is complete darkness until the glory of God shows up. Then, I came to realize with this dream, "ONLY GOD CAN BRING THE LIGHT!!!!"

The revealing of God's glory was made known to the dark places of my soul that had been areas, where I had fear, rejection, insecurities, and more. These areas were the strongholds of my soul, where the enemy attacked me. My soul was saved the moment I accepted Christ Jesus. However, from the past injuries of the fruit of the tree of the knowledge of good and evil, my soul was bruised and had need to be rebuilt with the abundant life Jesus came to bring. (See John 10:10)

My structure, in some areas of my soul was immediately refashioned in the truth of God, as I knew of salvation and my love for Jesus. However, the areas in which my soul still had strongholds, the truth of God's Word had not penetrated and brought the Light! The areas where the strongholds of the enemy were operative, were trying to cling to the old structure because my mind had not been renewed by the power of the Word in those particular areas. It was these areas of strongholds trying to hold me to that old structure that needed the light of God's truth.

The white eyelet dress represented two things. First the white represented the righteousness of Christ Jesus. Eyelet is a play on word where we see two words "eye" and "let."

"33 No one after lighting a lamp puts it in a cellar or crypt or under a bushel measure, but on a lampstand, that those who are coming in may see the light. 34 YOUR EYE IS THE LAMP of your body; when your eye (your conscience) is sound and fulfilling its office, your whole body is full of light; but when it is not sound and is not fulfilling its office, your body is full of darkness. 35 Be careful, therefore, that the light that is in you is not darkness. 36 If then your entire body is illuminated, having no part dark, it will be wholly bright [with light], as when a lamp with its bright rays gives you light." Luke 11:33-36 Amp

The "eye" is the lamp, and I had to "let" the lamp fulfill its office and do its work. The eye here represents the conscience of man (heart and mind), where there is an active work on our part, to seek God in His Word. As we continually are devoted to reading the Word of God and seeking Him, then the light of truth goes into our soul (heart and mind). Our duty is to carry the light of truth into our soul, partaking of that truth and trusting the working of truth in us.

The lamp was being carried out into the rest of my soul (body) where the darkness could not stay. Places where I did not have freedom in my soul were about to see the brightness of Gods' Light, the Word of God! I was not keeping the lamp of God's word veiled, but rather taking it throughout my entire soul, where I would eat on the Word of God to let the light of truth come into places of darkness and overcome the enemy of my soul! My entire body was being ILLUMINATED by the brightness of the Light of Jesus Christ!

"28 For You cause my lamp to be lighted and to shine; the Lord my God illumines my darkness." Psalm 18:28 Amp

"For the commandment is a lamp, and the whole teaching [of the law] is light, and reproofs of discipline are the way of life," Proverbs 6:23 Amp

"27 The spirit of man [that factor in human personality which proceeds immediately from God] is the lamp of the Lord, searching all his innermost parts." Proverbs 20:27 Amp

God revealed that my spirit being born from above was a lamp and light of the Lord that was searching my innermost parts. It is our spirit that is born from above, with the Word of God and Holy Spirit that causes our soul to be renovated, as we receive illumination from the Father.

The word "illuminated" in Luke 11:36 actually means, "to be full of light."[xi] Jesus said it was the "eye" that was the light (lamp) of the body. Eye here in Greek is *ophthalmos* pronounced *of-thäl-mo's* meaning "the eye, vision and sight."[xii] This comes from the root word meaning "to gaze, see, look, and watch."[xiii] Whatever it is that we give our time and attention to, what we gaze on, is manifested in our soul.

Where we had been under the first Adam before in darkness, we gazed on the things of this world. Now being in Christ Jesus, as we gaze upon the Word of God, every area of our soul that has been affected by the old structure is exposed and then overtaken by the Light of Truth. This is the process where scripture says that we are to work out our own salvation in fear and in trembling.

"12 Therefore, my dear ones, as you have always obeyed [my suggestions], so now, not only [with the enthusiasm you would show] in my presence but much more because I am absent, WORK OUT (CULTIVATE, CARRY OUT TO THE GOAL, AND FULLY COMPLETE) YOUR OWN SALVATION WITH REVERENCE AND AWE AND TREMBLING (SELF-DISTRUST, WITH SERIOUS CAUTION, TENDERNESS OF CONSCIENCE, WATCHFULNESS AGAINST TEMPTATION, TIMIDLY SHRINKING FROM WHATEVER MIGHT OFFEND GOD AND DISCREDIT THE NAME OF CHRIST). 13 [Not in your own strength] for it is God Who is all the while effectually at work in you [energizing and creating in you the power and desire], both to will and to work for His good pleasure and satisfaction and delight." Philippians 2:12-13 Amp

Paul exhorted the saints of Philippi to work out their own salvation being alert and watchful against temptations, with a tenderness of their conscience. This conscience represents the eye here in Philippians 2:12. When the conscience desires and delights in the light, then we are carrying that candle of God's Word throughout our soul. Thus, the conscience is the framework on which God would build and attach the structure of the Light. This is no different from our bones being the framework to attach muscles. God the Father formed us by the means of having a conscience (soul) where He would be able to bring the richness of HIS Light, so that it would permeate throughout our person.

You have heard many times when people commit horrible acts, the saying that they "must not have a conscience." Those who do not have a "conscience" of light show forth the fruits of death, and display this truth that the conscience is the framework that God builds upon.

Therefore, the conscience (soul) is the lamp of the body when we come into the Light of Christ Jesus. The "lamp" mentioned in Luke 11:36 is the Greek word *lychnos* pronounced *lü'kh-nos* meaning "a portable lamp or illuminator, candle and light."[xiv] As the light of God's truth permeates your soul (conscience) then it carries it throughout, illuminating the truth of God's Word that uproots, tears down and destroys the strongholds of the enemy.

The candle in my dream represented the light of God's truth, indicating that my "eye" was sound. I "LET" (eye-let dress) my "eye" (conscience) receive the STRUCTURE of the LIGHT by focusing on the Word! My soul was receptive to the light of God's truth because I hungered for the light. (My mind was sound and fulfilling its office/duty). This saints is how we workout our salvation in fear and in trembling.

Chapter 2 The Secret Garden

To gain understanding about the Eye being the Lamp of the Body, which represents our soul receiving the light of God's truth, we will see this through the analogy provided in scripture, as we are compared to a GARDEN. After God formed Adam, He put a framework in the earth, which would surround Adam's life. We see this in Genesis.

"15 And the Lord God took the man and put him in the Garden of Eden to tend and guard and keep it. 16 And the Lord God commanded the man, saying, You may freely eat of every tree of the garden; 17 But of the tree of the knowledge of good and evil and blessing and calamity you shall not eat, for in the day that you eat of it you shall surely die." Genesis 2:15-17 Amp

Here, we see that God put Adam in the GARDEN OF EDEN. Eden in Hebrew means "delight and pleasure." It was this garden that Adam was instructed to "tend and guard." The Hebrew word used for "tend and guard," is `abad pronounced *ä vad'* meaning "serve, dress, husbandman, keep, labor, execute, worshipper, be servant, etc."[xv] Adam's duty was simply to watch over the garden, which represented that which He worshipped. Likewise, the fruit of our labors always show forth what or Who we worship.

In this process Adam was instructed not to eat of a specific tree, which was the tree of the knowledge of good and evil; with it came death. As Adam dwelled in this framework his purpose on earth was to be fruitful and multiply and to take dominion. That ruling power and authority would manifest itself as Adam would first and foremost tend and guard the garden. He was to serve and labor in the garden of God's delight.

When temptation came in the form of the serpent, it distracted Adam from the framework in which God surrounded him, that of God's delight. As Adam and Eve's mind wondered, giving their ear to the serpent, they were beguiled because their gaze no longer was the garden, which they were given, but now their gaze turned to the tree of the knowledge of good and evil.

Because they turned their gaze upon the tree of the knowledge of good and evil, their conscience was now susceptible to temptation that did a work in their heart, causing them to stop the tending of their garden. They gave their conscience over to the availability of satan, which in turn brought in a new structure, bearing fruit of death. As they did not tend the garden, they did not fulfill their office (duty) of what God called them. Instead they gave their office (duty) to something else, which took root in their soul and caused them to partake of the tree that brought death.

The fruitfulness, dominion and multiplication Adam was called to, first of all began in the Garden of Eden. Here, as we look at the Garden of Eden, we see a representation of the soul of man, to do one thing "delight and take pleasure in the Lord." This delight and pleasure represents worship. What we worship we delight ourselves in, giving pleasure to do what it is that we delight.

Therefore, as Adam and Eve were now given over to the tree of the knowledge of good and evil, their delight changed from that of the Lord to the things of this world. The seed of the enemy would now spread and pollute their purity, providing knowledge of that which they were to never know.

We see the prophetic restoration of this garden throughout scriptures in both the Old and New Testaments.

"They shall come and sing aloud on the height of Zion and shall flow together and be radiant with joy over the goodness of the Lord—for the corn, for the juice [of the grape], for the oil, and for the young of the flock and the herd. AND THEIR LIFE SHALL BE LIKE A WATERED GARDEN, and they shall not sorrow or languish any more at all." Jeremiah 31:12 Amp

The life of God's people, were to be a "watered garden." The word "life" here in Hebrew is *nephesh* pronounced *neh' fesh* meaning "living creature, breath, soul, body, desire, heart, pleasure, tablet, etc."[xvi] "Water" here in Jeremiah 31:12 is the Hebrew word *raveh* pronounced *rä veh'* meaning, "sated with drink, drunkenness and watered."[xvii] The root word for water means, "to bathe, make drunk, fill, satiate, abundantly satisfy, soak and water abundantly."[xviii] Therefore, the well-watered garden represents a soul that is soaking up the Word, hungering and thirsting for righteousness. It is this soul that is continually made full, being satisfied, in the power of God's truth.

"12 A garden enclosed and barred is my sister, my [promised] bride—a spring shut up, a fountain sealed. 13 Your shoots are an orchard of pomegranates or a paradise with precious fruits, henna with spikenard plants, 14 Spikenard and saffron, calamus and cinnamon, with all trees of frankincense, myrrh, and aloes, with all the chief spices. 15 You are a fountain

[springing up] in a garden, a well of living waters, and flowing streams from Lebanon. 16 [You have called me a garden, she said] Oh, I pray that the [cold] north wind and the [soft] south wind may blow upon my garden, that its spices may flow out [in abundance for you in whom my soul delights]. Let my beloved come into his garden and eat its choicest fruits." Song of Solomon 4:12-16 Amp

When we look further at the well-watered garden, we see a more detailed description in Song of Solomon 4. She is a garden that is enclosed with protection as she is shut up and sealed. That sealing represents the sealing of our heart by Holy Spirit, Who is our guarantee unto the day of salvation. (See Ephesians 1:13) The different spices that flow from her, have great depths of representation that I get into in the "Song of Solomon 8:6-7 Army is Rising" book. With the Shulammite being shut up only for her Lover, she has now become a fountain that is springing up in a garden, which is a well of living waters. The living waters represents the life of Christ Jesus in us, which is by Holy Spirit, where we are now being satiated by the anointing of God's Word in us.

The streams for this garden are flowing from Lebanon. Lebanon in Hebrew means "white mountain and whiteness."[xix] The root word to Lebanon is the Hebrew word *lĕbab* pronounced *lev av'* meaning "HEART!"[xx] The living waters that water the garden then flow through the heart or can we say the soul. We have a duty to fulfill our office, which is to water the garden. The watering comes, as we are hungry and thirsty for righteousness, which results because we are in fellowship with the Word of God. When we stop watering the garden, then our pleasure has grown cold in the things of God and desires more of the things that are of this world.

As the Shulammite calls forth the north wind and south wind, we see the hungry soul crying out for more of Holy Spirit, and it is here that God causes the door to be opened. This well-watered Garden has now become a vineyard for her Lover, where He eats of its richest fruits. These fruits represent fruits of righteousness, which we give to the Father. (See 1 Philippians 1:11)

"I have come into my garden, my sister, my [promised] bride; I have gathered my myrrh with my balsam and spice [from your sweet words I have gathered the richest perfumes and spices]. I have eaten my honeycomb with my honey; I have drunk my wine with my milk. Eat, O friends [feast on, O revelers of the palace; you can never make my lover disloyal to me]! Drink, yes, drink abundantly of love, O precious one [for now I know you are mine, irrevocably mine! With his confident words still thrilling her heart, through the lattice she saw her shepherd turn away and disappear into the night]." Song of Solomon 5:1 Amp

We see here with Song of Solomon 5:1 that the Bridegroom has now come into the garden, which represents the light of Christ Jesus going throughout the soul. As He comes into the garden, he eats the honeycomb with honey, indicating the richness of His Word. He then drinks His wine with His milk. I have taught on the wine and milk in great detail in "God's Fire Wall School of the Prophets Session 1 Elohim." The wine represents the righteousness of Christ Jesus and the milk represents the anointing. Therefore, here we see the fellowship of the Word of God that is now providing a structure in our soul, through the inner connected parts, bringing wholeness, by the anointing of righteousness. The fellowship of God's Word produces "righteousness" and brings the "anointing."

"8 He who plants and he who waters are equal (one in aim, of the same importance and esteem), yet each shall receive his own reward (wages), according to his own labor. 9 For we are fellow workmen (joint promoters, laborers together) with and for God; YOU ARE GOD'S GARDEN AND VINEYARD AND FIELD UNDER CULTIVATION, [YOU ARE] GOD'S BUILDING. 10 According to the grace (the special endowment for my task) of God bestowed on me, like a skillful architect and master builder I laid [the] foundation, and now another [man] is building upon it. But let each [man] be careful how he builds upon it," 1 Corinthians 3:8-10 Amp

Paul the apostle tells the church of Corinth that they are God's garden, which is under cultivation and that God is the One, Who is building it. All these representations of our soul being the garden of God's delight brings us to the focus of the areas of our soul being renewed by God's Word.

Chapter 3 Revealing The Light

I do have a history of working with the seriously mentally ill in geriatrics, adults, and children. I took my licensure test for my graduate license (LGSW) in 2000 and worked with the seriously mentally ill (SMI). In the past, I looked at the medical model and saw through my own work, that success in treatment was sporadic for the SMI population. It was at that time, I discovered that medicine could not cure what ailed man's soul.

In my past professional career I worked with adults that have been in satanic ritual abuse (SRA), as well as multiple personalities (dissociative disorder), different personality disorders (histrionic, borderline, obsessive compulsive, etc.), schizophrenia, bipolar (manic depressive), psychotic, etc. Therefore, my exposure to the different mental health diagnosis has been varied. In my mid twenties, I worked in an adult day care with the SMI population. There were about 20-25 people on a given day that would be at the daycare. When I had time, I would go to the different patients getting information on what exactly occurred when they noticed they had an SMI.

It was as though God afforded me an opportunity to simply inquire and receive understanding as to what prompted this mental disease. As I talked to two people, a man and woman in their mid thirties, who were schizophrenic, I knew there had to be demonic oppression from what they described. Their soul was in torment continually by satan and his demons and I could see their desperation to be healed. The medicine seemed to help their existence but not ease the pain in their soul. The things they described were so satanic in nature that it was hard for me to comprehend how they could maintain any type of a life.

As I got older, I continued working with the mentally ill in my specialty of geriatrics, adult out patient psychiatry, and then later worked in therapeutic foster care with children. Each age group seemed to be affected the same way; they each wanted their pain to end and the medicines they were on had not removed the pain within the inner part of their soul. It was through this process of working in mental health, as well as in ministry that God began to reveal things about the soul of man.

No matter where I turned, in both the profession as well as in ministry, I found those who had dissociative disorder, schizophrenia, personality disorders and those in satanic ritual abuse, were drawn to me. Somehow God would bring people in my path that needed more than what medicine could offer. It was as though they knew that I had something to offer that would ease their pain.

After reading secular books from therapists who dealt with the dissociative disorder, I received more understanding from God. I discovered that a person's soul (mind and heart) can only take so much, and our Father knowing this, made our mind so incredibly complex that when something happens more than we can bear, our soul shuts that out in its own "file" so to speak. The soul compartmentalizes (shuts it in its own file in the soul) the evil thing, which has occurred, in order that the person can survive. If the soul did not do this, it would be too much for the person and they would not be able to survive it. We see this a lot with children who are molested and people who are severely abused.

As a result, the places in our soul, which have been in bondage to darkness and the enemy's torment, have been separated inside of the soul, in order that the person can endure. It is with God's Word and His grace by Holy Spirit, that He brings the Light of Christ Jesus into that area of the soul, not only to heal it but also to remove the memory. This negative memory is a reproach of the enemy on the soul (heart and mind). As the reproach is removed it is uprooted out of the mind of the person. (We will get into this more in book 2 "Healing of the Soul – The Wind").

This is not only relative to people with multiple personality disorder (dissociative disorder), but to each individual. God has afforded me the gift of working with the mentally ill so that I would gain better insight and understanding by Holy Spirit. The wounds of man's soul is a result of the enemy bruising us, in order to control and manipulate our every thought and action. We know our only tool to fight this battle is the Word of God!

There are areas of our soul that might be in bondage, needing the Light of Christ Jesus, which brings forth God's truth so that healing can take place. When I refer to "the Light" of Christ Jesus, I am directly referring to the "Word of God." There is some dangerous healing of the soul ministry that says to "call in the light." However, the only true light that is not of darkness is the Word of God, Christ Jesus! What truly grieved me with this false ministry that has people continually calling in "the light," is that one lady in particular told the false teacher it did not work and she was now in more pain than before. The reason the woman had pain in her soul, was because a door where there was darkness was opened. As a result, instead of bringing the true "Light," the Word of God into her soul, the opposite was occurring. The door that was opened, where darkness had been dormant, no longer was shut, but instead began flooding her soul.

The response given by the false teacher to this hurting soul was "continue to call in the light and it will go away." I wanted to scream! The false teacher did not see the damage she was doing to this woman in particular, nor to those who were reading and listening to her material. Instead she took something that became popular by labeling it "healing of the soul" and using a phrase to "call in the light" like a partaker of Woodstock in the 1960s, which seemed like nothing but "New Age."

In addition, we do not go into our past or look at our childhood but are told instead to press onward to the prize of the high call. Ministries that go through your childhood and your past are doing more damage than good; it is only God Almighty that goes into our past and He goes there to remove that which is a reproach.

If a ministry goes into a person's past they actually can cause wounds where the person can be traumatized again, resulting in worse behavioral problems and inability to effectively overcome. The only way, in which we are healed (set free and delivered) is by THE WORD OF GOD!!! It is not by calling in light or doing guided imagery into our past; that is all a source of divination. The way in which we are set free and healed is clearly delineated in scripture. God's Word that pierces our soul to bring the Light of Christ Jesus, the power of the Word, is what heals us! (See John 1:5)

"THE LAW OF THE LORD IS PERFECT, RESTORING THE [WHOLE] PERSON; the testimony of the Lord is sure, making wise the simple." Psalm 19:7 Amp

The Word of God is the Law of truth, and we fulfill the law as we walk in the love of Christ Jesus. (See Galatians 5:14) God's perfect love in us fulfills the law and we are not under it because of the finished work of Christ, instead we are under God's marvelous grace. As we look at scripture here when we read from the psalmist who says, "God's law is perfect restoring the whole person," it can be read, as "God's Word is perfect, restoring the whole person." The word "restore" here in Hebrew *shuwb* pronounced *shüv* means, "to turn back, to circumcise, feed, lay down, cause to answer, fetch, pull in again, recompense, recover, relieve, requite, rescue, restore, reverse, reward, take back off, etc."[xxi] Therefore, the Word of God turns us back, pulling us in to take off of us that which the enemy has placed on us, as God rescues and restores us, giving us a circumcised heart to dwell in His rest. This saint of God is a lot of work in this one word "restore". We see this in the circumcision in Hebrews 4:12 that brings restoration.

"12 For the Word that God speaks is alive and full of power [making it active, operative, energizing, and effective]; it is sharper than any two-edged sword, penetrating to the dividing line of the breath of life (soul) and [the immortal] spirit, and of joints and marrow [of the deepest parts of our nature], exposing and sifting and analyzing and judging the very thoughts and purposes of the heart." Hebrews 4:12 Amp

The Word of God is the surgical instrument that circumcises the heart. "Word" here in Greek is *logos* pronounced *lo'-gos* meaning "something said (including a thought), reasoning (the mental faculty), motive, by extension, a computation, the Divine Expression in Christ, mouth, preaching, doctrine, fame, speech, talk, word, etc."[xxii] The root word for *logos* is *legō* pronounced *legō* meaning "to lay forth."[xxiii]

God gave me a great analogy when it comes to the word "logos." He showed me the Lego blocks that my sons had while they were growing up. They would buy a box of Legos that had an entire city in it. It had everything in the box that could build people, cars, buildings and anything else imaginable. As they would place a Lego on top of another one, they were able to build a car, then a building, and in time, an entire city. Likewise, the Word of God builds up the Holy City that is within, by the truth in God's Word, which restores us. We then see who we were always meant to be, as the Word builds us up in the Last Adam's structure.

Lego in Greek means, "to lay forth." As Jesus was the *Logos* (the Word), He came to *Lego* (lay forth) the Father! Jesus came to show us the Father. (See John 14:8-21)

"31 So Jesus said to those Jews who had believed in Him, If you abide in My word [hold fast to My teachings and live in accordance with them], you are truly My disciples. 32 And you will know the Truth, and the Truth will set you free." John 8:31-32 Amp

Jesus came to show us the Truth and it would be the Truth of Who the Father is, which would restore us. The word truth from John 8:32 is the Greek Word *alētheia* pronounced *ä-lā'-thā-ä* and is a noun meaning "truth, truly and true."[xxiv] The Greek word that truth comes from is a the adjective *alēthēs* pronounced *ä-lā-thā's* meaning "true, truly and truth." It has the same meanings as the actual word of truth, but the only difference is the first one is a noun (person, place or thing) and the second one is an adjective describing something or someone. The Word of God is truth (a thing and a Person) and all that it does is true (the description/adjective).

This is what is going to blow your mind; the adjective form of the word for "truth" reveals the two Greek Words that compose it. The first word that helps compose the word "truth" is *Alpha,* which of course means the first and beginning. Jesus is the Alpha and the Omega; He is the Beginning and the End. The second word that composes the word "truth," is the Greek word *lanthanō* pronounced *län-thā'-nō* meaning "to lie hid, be hid, be ignorant of and unawares."[xxv] Thus the Word is the truth of Alpha (Jesus) who lies hidden! This is Mark 4:21-24, where we see a Lamp that is brought into a room!

"21 And He said to them, Is the lamp brought in to be put under a peck measure or under a bed, and not [to be put] on the lampstand? 22 [Things are hidden temporarily only as a means to revelation.] For there is nothing hidden except to be revealed, nor is anything [temporarily] kept secret except in order that it may be made known. 23 If any man has ears to hear, let him be listening and let him perceive and comprehend. 24 And He said to them, Be careful what you are hearing. The measure [of thought and study] you give [to the truth you hear] will be the measure [of virtue and knowledge] that comes back to you—and more [besides] will be given to you who hear." Mark 4:21-24 Amp

The lamp is brought into a room, to be put on the lampstand (a place where light can fill the room). Likewise, the Light of God comes by Holy Spirit, to reveal that which has been hidden in the seed of His Word. God's Word is that seed that is planted in our soul as we see in the parable of Mark 4, which I go into detail in Session 1 of "God's Fire Wall School of the Prophets." As the Word in us is planted and begins to try and test us, it brings forth the revealing of ALPHA (JESUS) that is hidden in Scripture!

As Scripture is opened up to us, we see Jesus laying forth the Father. The Word, reveals THE LIGHT OF GOD THAT IS FROM ETERNITY, THE LIGHT FROM THE BEGINNING!!! This is Genesis 1:3 where God's light continually shines from eternity to reveal the eternal God. The Light of God came to illuminate man, revealing the Divine Expression of Christ Jesus.

"9 There it was—the true Light [was then] coming into the world [the genuine, perfect, steadfast Light] that illumines every person." John 1:9 Amp

Chapter 4 The Two Trees

"4 In Him was Life, and the Life was the Light of men." John 1:4 Amp

In Jesus was LIFE and that LIFE was the LIGHT of men! The word "life" here in Greek is *zōē* pronounced *zō-ā'* meaning "life."[xxvi] In the Life of Jesus we see the divine expression of the Light of God. Therefore, in order to comprehend the "light of truth" we have to see where it stems, which is from the Life of Jesus Christ. He came to bring life and life abundantly. (See John 10:10) This Life represents the Tree of Life in the Garden of Eden. We see the Tree of Life, not only in Genesis 2:9 but in Revelation 22:2, as well.

"2 Through the middle of the broadway of the city; also, on either side of the river was the tree of life with its twelve varieties of fruit, yielding each month its fresh crop; and the leaves of the tree were for the healing and the restoration of the nations." Revelation 22:2 Amp

The Tree of Life is by the river that flows from God's throne. On the Tree of Life are leaves, which have healing and restoration to heal the nations. I teach in great length on Revelation 22:2 in the watchman book "Revelation 22:2 The Tree of Life – God's Life Guards." Here, we see that the tree of life has leaves that bring healing and restoration to nations. These leaves represent the Anointed Word of God given to His people, which restore their soul.

As in the Garden of Eden, there is the Tree of Life and the tree of the knowledge of good and evil, with which we have issue within our own hearts. By looking at the Garden of Eden, we see how we are to contend as we continually choose from the tree we will eat. As we look at the soul deeper we will see the garden, which lies hidden and the different means by which the enemy does, and does not have access to our soul. The means by which we will examine this will be between the two trees of the Garden of Eden, which is the Tree of Life and the tree of the knowledge of good and evil.

Like Eden, God shows us there is the tree of the knowledge of good and evil and the Tree of Life that exists in our soul, but that it is our choice as to which tree we will eat of. As Adam and Eve chose to eat from the tree of the knowledge of good and evil, they "let" their conscience (eye) be beguiled by the serpent. They did not heed the Word of God and after they ate of the fruit they saw that they were naked.

The word "naked," in Genesis 2:25, which was before they ate of the tree of the knowledge of good and evil, is different than the word "naked" used after they ate of it in Genesis 3:7.

"And the man and his wife were both naked and were not embarrassed or ashamed in each other's presence." Genesis 2:25 Amp

"Then the eyes of them both were opened, and they knew that they were naked; and they sewed fig leaves together and made themselves apronlike girdles." Genesis 3:7 Amp

The first word "naked" in Genesis 2:25 means to be naked as if to be bare, and the second word used for "naked" used in Genesis 3:7 actually means "nudity and nakedness," so the focus in the second word for "naked" amplifies the FLESH.

Moreover, the second word for "naked" exposes the chaos operative, in our lives. I will get into more detail with the Hebrew letters, in year 3 of God's Fire Wall School of the Prophets that will begin with book 19 of the series. However, I wanted to show you the depth of richness that the Hebrew letters reveal between these two words for "naked."

When we look at the ancient Hebrew letters that are pre-Canaanite, they are composed of pictures that are symbols. You have heard the saying a picture is worth a thousand words. To show you the distinctions between the two words for naked in Hebrew, by looking at the Hebrew letters we obtain better understanding.

The word for naked where Adam and Eve were ashamed in Genesis 3:7, is the Hebrew word `eyrom pronounced ā rōm', the Hebrew letters which compose it are Ayin, Yood, Resh and Mem.[xxvii] The ancient symbol of the Hebrew letter "Ayin" is the symbol of an eye, meaning, "to see, know and experience." The ancient symbol for the Hebrew letter "Yood" is the symbol of an arm at work meaning, "works, make and deed." Next, the ancient symbol for the Hebrew letter "Resh," is the ancient symbol of a man's face and means "head, highest and person." Finally, The ancient symbol for the Hebrew letter Mem is water and means "massive" in the positive, as well as "chaos" in the negative. Also, with the ancient Hebrew letter Mem it indicates that water floods us. Therefore, the word picture you have here for naked is **"SEEING THE WORKS AND DEEDS OF CHAOS THAT MASSIVELY FLOOD YOUR PERSON."** All the enemy can do is come against God's order (truth) and bring chaos. When the enemy brings this chaos into our mind and we listen to him, we are eating of the tree of the knowledge of good and evil.

Naked in Genesis 2:25 where Adam and Eve were naked and unashamed is the Hebrew word `arowm pronounced ä rōm' and the Hebrew letters that compose this word are Ayin, Resh, Vav and Mem.[xxviii] There is only one difference between these two Hebrew words, because the one in Genesis 3:7 has the Hebrew letter "Yood" in it, and this one has the Hebrew letter "Vav." Again Ayin represents the eye meaning, "to see, know and experience," and Resh represents a face meaning "head, highest and person." Finally Mem represents water meaning "massive" and "chaos." Now we see the huge difference with the Hebrew letter "Vav" in this word for naked. "Vav" is the ancient symbol of a nail or peg and means "to add and secure." Therefore the word picture you have for the Hebrew word naked in Genesis 2:25 is **"EXPERIENCING THE MOST HIGH'S NAIL (THE WORK OF THE CROSS) THAT ADDS AND SECURES GOD'S MASSIVENESS."**

The Genesis 2:25 naked reveals that Adam and Eve were cloaked and covered by God! Because God was their covering, they knew not of their own nakedness. It was when the covering of God was removed, by eating the fruit of the tree of the knowledge of good and evil that things changed. Their gaze changed and was no longer fulfilling the office of God but instead was allowing the fruit of death to spread like a spiritual disease throughout their soul, causing chaos on every turn.

When our soul is in that place where we are not under the Hebrews 4:12 covering of God, which is the Tree of Life that operates and circumcises our heart, it is under the other tree of the knowledge of good and evil. As a result of being under the tree of the knowledge of good and evil, our eyes are exposed to the grossness of all that is in this world.

As we set our gaze upon things of this world, it becomes our reality. As a result, we feel the chaos in areas that have not been set apart unto "life;" it is in these places of our soul that the enemy manipulates us. As a result, we end up behaving in the pattern of that chaos, which we believe to be our reality.

The Word of God diverts us from eating of the tree of the knowledge of good and evil so we do not partake of it, and instead brings His covering of love over our nakedness where we are unashamed; our aim is to walk in God's Love.

"I appeal to you therefore, brethren, and beg of you in view of [all] the mercies of God, to make a decisive dedication of your bodies [presenting all your members and faculties] as a living sacrifice, holy (devoted, consecrated) and well pleasing to God, which is your reasonable (rational, intelligent) service and spiritual worship. 2 Do not be conformed to this world (this age), [fashioned after and adapted to its external, superficial customs], but be transformed (changed) by the [entire] renewal of your mind [by its new ideals and its new attitude], so that you may prove [for yourselves] what is the good and acceptable and perfect will of God, even the thing which is good and acceptable and perfect [in His sight for you]." Romans 12:1-2 Amp

Offering our body as a living sacrifice is choosing to eat of the Tree of Life and allowing that structure of truth to bring the Light of Jesus Christ into our soul, providing renewal. As we are transformed and renewed in our mind, providing the framework from the Last Adam, our mind is transformed and renewed in that area. Once the Word comes to an area of our soul that had the provision of the tree of the knowledge of good and evil feeding it, it uproots the tree that brings death, by tearing it down and destroying it.

Again, this can be compared to renovating a home that is filled with mold and rotted throughout. The Word of God would be like the construction worker that sees what is wrong with the house. Instead of keeping something that would be a detriment to the home, like rotted wood or mold, the construction worker pulls it out of the house and replaces it with something new and better. The tree of the knowledge of good and evil can be compared to the rotted wood or mold. The Word of God builds us up in the Light of God's glory and our soul is no longer torn apart and desolate but instead is BUILT UP!

This evidence is seen in my own life when God delivered me from alcohol. The reason I stayed bound up in alcohol was because I continually ate of the tree of the knowledge of good and evil. Where my soul ached, and my nakedness was evident, I was bound up in shame and wanted to medicate that shame by drinking.

The only way the enemy can hold us bondage, as with Adam and Eve, is by causing us to feel "shame." When we feel shame we do not run to God but rather run away from Him. It's a place where our soul gets on a rollercoaster of shame and cannot find the means by which to get off. The shame that has us bound causes us to be given over to behaviors that further bring even more shame. These areas of continual struggles with shame in our life are the indicator that we are eating of the tree of the knowledge of good and evil in that particular place of our soul.

The conformity of the world in Romans 12:2 is representative of the tree of the knowledge of good and evil. However, when we have a renewed mind in the truth of God's Word, we are instead eating of the Tree of Life.

The word transformed in Greek for Romans 12:2 is *metamorphoō* pronounced *me-tä-mor-fo'-ō* meaning, "change, transfigure and transform."[xxix] This word is composed of two Greek words, with the first one meaning something that is "joined" to bring change, because of the relation of the new fellowship. The second word, which composes transformed in Greek means "to fashion." Therefore, the revealing of this Greek word is that when the "Word of God" is joined to us, it brings about a change, by fashioning us into the glory of God.

This truly is the revealing of how a caterpillar turns into a butterfly. The caterpillar represents the old nature, and what is interesting is the location the caterpillar goes to for the change to take place. Where do caterpillars make their cocoons? They make their cocoons on a TREE! In addition as we see the word "caterpillar" it is easy to see two words in the midst of it, which are "cater" and "pillar." Remember that Zion means, "pillar," and we are of the spiritual Zion as we are born from above! The word "cater" actually means to "provide food and drink." Thus, as we get the food and drink of God's Word from the Tree of Life, His pillar of truth is seen in us.

When we are added and secured to the Tree of Life, it keeps our vision single and upon the Tree of Life. Then as we are joined to the Tree of Life, God brings forth His fashion, which is the image of Christ Jesus! (See 2 Corinthians 3:18)

The transformation in our person takes place by the renewing of our mind. "Renewal" in Romans 12:2 is the Greek word *anakainōsis* pronounced *ä-nä-kī'-nō-sēs* meaning "renovation and renewing."[xxx] The renovation of the soul comes by renovating the mind!

MY PERSONAL ENCOUNTER

When I was around 19 years old I became involved with a man my mother warned me of, whom she believed was demon possessed. As a result of my rebellion, I did not heed my parents' counsel and married the man. After I married him, one thing led to another where I found myself tortured beyond measure; he began abusing me. I have been married three times altogether, with this being my first marriage in the 1980s and then marrying my second husband in the 1990s, who I was with for seven years before he left the boys and I. Finally, God brought Rich into my life in 2001 and we have been married for 15 years, with yesterday (December 22nd) being our 15th year anniversary. I truly felt like that Samaritan woman at the well, whom Jesus prophesied to.

I have not seen any movie to date that touched on the level of abuse I endured in that brief 9-month marriage in the 1980s to that man who was demon possessed. God's grace removed me from that circumstance when I had a window of opportunity to get out of the house. Usually, he locked me in the house as a prisoner with a dead bolt lock. When he locked the door, he would also remove the phone, so I could not contact anyone (this was in mid 1980s so there were no cell phones).

During this time of abuse, I worked part time at a jewelry store, in a place where he would keep a constant watch over me. Every time I got a paycheck I was required to hand it over to him lest he beat me. Most of the time I had an apple a day and maybe another vegetable. What made me angry is I saw him sitting outside the jewelry store where I worked, in the mall eating a pizza that he had bought with my money. When I would stand up for myself because of these frustrations I would get beat.

Now came the opportunity for me to be set free and it was the Lord God Who quickened me to get out; if I did not I knew that I would die. The night that I left my abuser God showed me what to do to get out safely. I saw him on the toilet, and knew that it was my only opportunity to run for the door. However, I was aware that if he knew I was planning to escape he would beat me up to the point of death. By this time I weighed 82-87 pounds soaking wet due to all the starvation he put me through. The only problem was that he had the key, which I needed to get in order to unlock the door.

I did only what I knew to do in my moment of opportunity, in order to get the key from him. I got a frying pan from the kitchen and did what I knew I had to in order to buy me time to get the key, which was to knock him on the head with it. This provided me "time" to escape as I reached for the key to run and unlock the door.

It was now 2 am in the morning after I hit him and ran out of the door. I began running up a hill for my life, and saw him coming after me angrier than I've ever seen him. It was at this point I knew that if he ever caught me I would be dead. What baffled me is that I was so emaciated and unnourished that I knew there was a greater strength in me causing me to run up this hill, which was about a quarter of a mile.

I ran as fast as I could, and when I got to the top of the hill I saw a policeman. As I reached the police car I collapsed crying out to the policeman "help me!" He saw my ex-husband in pursuit of me and asked me what I needed. I explained to the policeman what was going on and simply said I want to call my parents. My parents were 1 ½ hours away and every time I called them in the past, I had to do so while my ex-husband was sitting right beside me.

If I said one thing wrong he would make sure that I would not do it again by giving me a severe beating. Usually, he would take the phone out of the house where I could not call my parents while I was locked in there. The lock on the door was a dead bolt lock that could be locked on the outside and inside of the house. Therefore, when he left the house and locked me in I was basically in a prison. Also, when he returned home each day, he would come in the house and lock me in, keeping the key in his pocket.

When the cop allowed me to call my parents, they told me to come home. I wanted to go home so many times but my abuser was using my car and would not let me have it. With this information, the policeman went back with me to watch while I packed my things and left. What was so amazing is God not only had that policeman at the top of the hill at 2 am in the morning, but also he had my best friend at the time who lived 35 minutes away pass by that little gas station, where I was with the policeman! Only God could have coordinated the policeman being there and my friend driving by at that time. I remember my friend said three words while the policeman had my abuser distracted, she said "Robin go home." I knew that it was God speaking through her and it was then that He pulled me out of the hellhole I had been in.

Before, I was in relationship with the man who abused me, I had great confidence; I was a cheerleader, bold and fearless. However, 9 months with my first husband did enough damage to my soul that it took years for me to be made whole. I went through all kinds of counseling and could never find anything that would truly help bring peace to my soul. It was years later, when I came to the Word of God that healing began to come. Finally, I was able to apply God's Word to my soul and found that my soul had places of bondage and darkness.

This is what blew my mind; God shut down areas of my soul of the abuse from my first marriage, to a point that I could not remember the fact that I was ever abused! It was at this time in my life where I first "disassociated." God is so gracious and merciful that He knew I could not survive remembering the severity of what happened to me, so he allowed the fragmentation of that place of my soul and separated it from the rest of me. I know this might be hard to handle but you will see this further when we get into the book of Nehemiah. Because of my backsliding I was eating of the tree of the knowledge of good and evil that led me to making wrong decisions and experiencing death and destruction on every turn. My soul was a mess!

Before, discovering the power of God's Word, He graciously shut the tormenting memory off from the rest of my soul. One day while I was doing my bachelor internship for social work, my supervisor told me that she wanted to talk with me. (I want to preface this with saying this was about 4 years after I had left the abusive first husband and was now married to my second husband). We met weekly for our regular supervision, and I was thinking it must be our regular visit. As we sat down I had no clue what was about to take place and as best as I can describe, I will lay out the event. It is my hope that you will see how the soul operates so that you can see how complex our soul is, and how God's grace closes areas of our mind so that we can survive.

My supervisor told me that she wanted to talk with me about something that she had noticed. As I sat down across from my supervisor she gently asked, "Robin have you ever been abused?"

I replied to her "No."

She looked at me and said, "well some of your behaviors indicate to me that you have been abused." She began to list the behaviors and as I sat there it blew my mind that she was correct on all the signs I had been exhibiting.

I still was baffled while looking at my supervisor, and had one thought, which was, "that's odd." She probably thought I was looking at her like she had seven heads. As she discussed the matter further, she stated "when you walk up to me, you lift your hands together into your chest and while doing so point them down. She then said "you bend your back over a little bit, looking timid." As she continued, she further explained to me the way that I spoke and interacted with her were not normal. Now imagine if you were me, thinking you have never been abused, how crazy you would think this woman was if she was asking you this question and pointing out all these signs. I truly thought she had lost her mind.

As I continued to listen to her I was thinking, "Where in the world could this behavior be coming from because I know I have not been abused." I sat there and pondered thinking over and over in my mind, where this behavior would be attributed. THEN IT HIT ME!!!! It was at this moment everything, as I knew changed. The best description I can give is a child's closet. In many storylines you see the child that is cleaning up their room, and the way they clean it is to put everything in the closest.

When they finally shut the door, they hope that no one will ever open it; knowing that everything in the closet is going to come falling and spilling out. Their room looks clean to them and others, so that in their reality they believe it is clean. However, if you were to open the child's closet you would find that their room is far from clean and merely opening it up, launches all the stuff piled up in the closet across the room, as things come flying out.

Well, that is what happened to my soul after my first marriage. I stuffed all the abuse that occurred with my ex-husband behind a door in my soul that was not to be opened. The means by which I functioned in a somewhat normal life was because all of the abuse was piled up behind the shut door.

I never could have foreseen this shut door to my soul, which on this day was being opened. The door to my soul that had stuffed all the darkness, all the abuse, and all the demonic attacks, all of a sudden flew open and it was as though I was going to have a nervous breakdown. I started breathing hard and my body began to sweat and it was as though I saw a massive movie that was over 40 hours long in a 5 minute flash before my eyes; everything began to spill out, fall down, fly out of the door that had been closed for so long in my soul! I began to say in a loud voice "Oh my gosh!!!! Yes yes yes I was abused!!!!" I was stunned, overwhelmed, shocked, angry, and sad; you name it and most likely I felt it at that moment.

Now the whole matter was just a huge mess in my soul and I did not know what to do. Before when I didn't remember the abuse, I was perfectly fine and able to function throughout my day because I had shut out the trauma. However, once this door was opened I was a huge mess due to the emotions linked with the events that began to torment me over and over again.

I could see the knife put to my throat, the gun to my head, the horrible beatings over and over and over again not only in the home but in public places as well, where my ex threatened others who would try to intervene. My soul was in torment! I found myself perplexed and overwhelmed, as I did not know what to do, after discovering this information.

At this time I was in my second year of my second marriage to a medical student and still had a couple of years of college in order to complete my bachelors degree. I did go to church during this time every single week as my parents started creating the habit for me when I was a little girl. However, there was no wholeness or healing for what ailed my soul.

Moreover, with the relationship I had in my second marriage there was injury added to my soul making me feel even more deficient as a woman. That second marriage went for almost 7 years and ended up with him leaving me for another woman. My soul then was more damaged and injured, and as a result of the two relationships I was a complete basket case.

It was at this time of being a single mother and being desperate to end all of the pain, that I backslid and turned to alcohol to medicate all the pain and shame of my soul. I was naked and there was no one to cover me, or so I thought. It was in this time of desperation that God spoke to me in my inner man and told me to continually eat the Word.

As I began to eat the Word in my messed up state, where I was an alcoholic, fornicator, dysfunctional mess, God began to go through all the things that had been hidden in my soul that caused pain. Where I had places in which I had eaten of the tree of the knowledge of good and evil, the Word of God came in and began to destroy the stronghold. I was not totally set free by the time I met Rich but I was on the way to restoration.

I met Rich, "My Italian Man," which felt like a match made in heaven. The day we met I felt it was as though I had met him before in heaven, and God said "Robin this is Rich remember him when you get to earth."

That is the only way I can describe how it felt when I met him. Rich and I married in late 2001. God gave Rich the love of Christ Jesus, and grace to stay married to me while He began to work a deep inner healing in my soul. As I continued through the years in my marriage with Rich, God began giving me direction on specific scriptures to declare and meditate on in order to bring healing to my soul.

Within time, my soul began to be filled with such love from God that it felt as though God loved the hurt out of my soul. Before I knew it I could not recall the details of my past sexual, physical and emotional abuse. I COULD NOT REMEMBER!!!!!! GOD REMOVED THE REPROACH AND SHAME OF MY WIDOWHOOD. (See Isaiah 54:4) The widowhood represented the place of darkness that I sat in all those years listening to the lies of the enemy and eating of the tree of the knowledge of good and evil. Today I simply remember that I had been abused and to a measure of what I endured, but there are no details. I do not have the memories; God totally removed them all, which we will see in scripture. The only vivid memory I truly have with great detail is the day I was set free!!!!!!!!!

YOUR SOUL WILL BE MADE WHOLE

Maybe you did not experience what I did as it relates to past trauma and injury to your soul, but whether you did or not, your soul still has places it needs the light of God's truth. God brings the light of His truth in the midst of your darkness, in order to bring your soul healing and wholeness. When your soul receives healing and wholeness by God, You are able to walk in victory by the power of Holy Spirit. I teach on the baptism of Holy Spirit in "God's Fire Wall School of the Prophets Session 1 – Elohim."

God told me that as the Temple has three sections of the outer court, inner court (Holy Place) and the Holy of Holies, it is the same for us. The outer court is our body, which is visible. Our body has access to natural sunlight and the light of God's glory. The Holy Place represented the place in which we are filled by God's Spirit, and our spirit is born above, through the display of the light of the Menorah filling the Holy Place. However, the Most Holy Place (Holy of Holies) is hidden behind a curtain with the Ark of Covenant, and there is no light there except for God's presence; God is the Light of the Temple!

Holy Spirit showed me how the Holy of Holies was likened unto our soul, because there were places in our soul that were waiting on the light of Christ Jesus, the presence of God to break forth and fill us completely. As He gave me the dream of standing in the midst of the pillars to go out into the darkness and carry the light, He revealed the presence of God's glory in the soul of man. He revealed that when I was walking into the darkness with the candle of Light, I was bringing the presence of Christ Jesus; He is the Light of the world. Moreover, since my spirit was born from above it was also the light within my spirit that was taking His light to the rest of my soul.

In my dream, the gold bell was on my left arm. The left arm represented the arm of the flesh, but it was tied with scarlet ribbon, indicating the blood of Jesus. The blood of Jesus Christ was over all the works of flesh by the finished work of the cross. I was no longer bound to those works but instead had works of righteousness.

The gold bell represented the bells at the bottom of the high priest's robe, which he wore before walking into the Holy of Holies. God showed me that I am Holy as He is Holy but it is the revelation of Christ Jesus in me, the righteousness of Christ in me through the Word, which brings that light to the rest of my soul that has sat in darkness for such a great time.

God disclosed to me that it is difficult to sit in a dark place in your soul, in order to wait on Him to come. We come into that darkness not by our will but Holy Spirit leads us. Holy Spirit led Jesus into the Wilderness to overcome all the temptations of the enemy. Likewise, Holy Spirit knows when we have the power to overcome the enemy and in our trial it feels as though our soul is in darkness. God is the One Who knows what it is going to take to get us where He wants to take us. Therefore, as we wait on the light of God's glory we overcome that darkness that has warred in our soul.

During my trials and tribulation I chose not to run away from the darkness but rather to sit there with the Word, reading it over and over and over. As I continued to gaze at the Word of God in my darkness, the Light of God began to envelop and surround me. As I obeyed, God brought His glory making me holy, as He is Holy.

Again, God assured me that my husband in the dream, indicated Jesus the Bridegroom, Who would go with me into the places of darkness. God quickened me that as I remained still and waited on the Lord, He would renew my strength, and would come. Therefore, I pressed into this new revelation by Holy Spirit that the structure of my soul was created and designed by the Father through the Last Adam.

I knew God already healed me according to His Word, and I needed to wait on that healing. It was in 2001 that I agreed to this process, and over time God has brought the Light of Christ Jesus into the darkness to bring forth divine healing; His Word has made me whole, and restored me.

Before restoration occurred I had constant panic attacks and horrible anxiety. I could not be among other people because I had been so beaten down that I would get knots in my stomach sending me running to the bathroom.

My colon and digestive track were a mess from all the anxiety in my soul. There was no peace in my person, as I constantly fought a battle I thought I could never win. I felt uncomfortable in my own skin and did not want to live. However, as God began healing me, He breathed into me strength and love beyond anything of this earth that would not let me give up.

Over the past several years I have been in many deliverance meetings, have several deliverance books, and have sat in on several deliverance sessions helping others be set free. In this time it has been my privilege to witness God do amazing things in the lives of others.

Although I have witnessed deliverance through God's ministers I have also been a witness to His deliverance in my own life privately. God is so good and awesome that He delivered me on several occasions as He drove out demonic oppression that tormented my soul. He delivered me from bondages of the enemy that had kept my soul in places of darkness. When the day of deliverance came there was supernatural manifestation. I only share what the Father lets me because some of my encounters of deliverance are more than some can bear. God wants me to share a deliverance I experienced, where He drove the devil of fear out that was oppressing me.

Let me preface this testimony, with the fact that I have been in the Baptist Church for nearly 32 years of my life. At the age of 34 I was desperate and God led me to an Assembly of God church. On Resurrection Sunday of 2002 I was filled with Holy Spirit. Since that time, God has brought me through many peculiar circumstances I have yet to truly put into words. In the deliverances I would have from the Lord, He would visit me with a tangible weight of His presence and go into my soul and cut asunder the root of the enemy removing it fully.

When God did this on one occasion I was leaving the house going to workout at the gym. We lived around the corner from the gym, less than a quarter of a mile. I left the house feeling great, and as soon as I turned around the corner, suddenly I felt strange. It literally felt as though I was going to die; my whole body felt as though it was turning on me.

I felt a horrible weakness come on my person that caused me to tremble. As I grew worse physically, I pulled off the road and thought "God I am going to die." I reached for the phone in attempt to call Rich and tell him goodbye, since I had never experienced anything like this. Fear flooded my mind, as it could not comprehend what was occurring in my body and soul. I wanted to make sure I was right with God and others and be ready for what might come my way. My hands were so weak that I could not dial Rich's number and I became terrified, because now I am thinking I won't be able to tell him goodbye.

Then, I became so nauseated and my head began to slump over. At that moment a "glob" of mucus type stuff the size of a golf ball projected out of my mouth, as if it was being driven out. As the glob came out, my first thought was "OH GROSS!!!"

I had never seen anything like that before in my life. After my mind was trying to process what happened, I was then engulfed in the tangible presence of God! Holy Spirit flooded into my body and filled me with ecstasy and joy, where I felt myself being lifted up.

What occurred in my person was that the light of God's truth came into the darkness of my soul, where fear laid dormant and it uprooted that fear of man, as God flooded me with His love. I felt that demonic oppression in my stomach, where it lay hidden and this was the day where it would be ejected.

I have taught in our classes also how demonic spirits sometimes are resident within the belly. This day, that oppression that had been in my belly was uprooted by the Light of God to bring that thing all the way up from my stomach, through my digestive track and up through my throat to discharge this thing out of my mouth!!!! I have two words for this, "JUST WOW!"

In our soul, where we are eating of the tree of the knowledge of good and evil, God separates that as He did in Genesis 1, where He separated the light and darkness. He does it in order that the Tree of Life can inhabit our person (our garden) where we fellowship in the light of truth and this is the place where He dwells.

For example, a prostitute can be on the streets and someone with the light of God's truth ministers to her the Word of truth. When they minister to her the Word of truth, because she has so much knowledge of the tree of good and evil, those areas have to be separated in her soul so that the Holy Spirit can bring the Tree of Life to her garden, causing her to eat the fruit thereof. Although she might be set free in measure from that one encounter, she still has a process to go through in eating the Word of God and fellowshipping in the truth of that Word to see the transformation and renewal of her mind.

Likewise, any area where we eat of the tree of the knowledge of good and evil, whether or not we committed the sin or an evil act was committed against us, that area has to be separated and shut in, as we see that God's garden is shut up, with the Shulammite. It is no different for us; when we eat of the tree of the knowledge of good and evil, and are in bondage, it is shut up, awaiting the light of Truth to destroy the works of that tree and remove it from our person.

This is why some people are having areas in which they do not find themselves free and at times they feel schizophrenic. They have the Tree of Life in their garden as well as the tree of the knowledge of good and evil, but which tree are they tending? When you tend the wrong tree, then you put your gaze upon it and it is added to your person. It is for this reason to know the truth; the truth will set you free!

Chapter 5 Light Shines in the Darkness

Whatever bondage, captivity, or pain that is in your soul (mind and heart) will come out by the grace of God's Word. There have been times where I received healing and deliverance to my soul from ungodly grief and sorrow by crying uncontrollably off and on for hours. After I finished crying I felt like a new person, and my soul no longer hurt.

Presently, anytime there is injury against my soul where the enemy would try and harm me through another person, God immediately removes it. I find myself in these moments where someone has spoken something from the pit of hell over me, and if I let my defenses down and it tries to come into my soul, I immediately go into travail and begin weeping. After I am finished weeping it is as though this weight is lifted off of my shoulder and the reproach of the enemy's curse is lifted off of me. It feels like a cloak of heaviness when this happens. Once God removes the ungodly cloak, and binds my heart by the Spirit of the Lord, He then places a garment of His praise over me.

Our soul is a city; becoming a place of habitation. As God's glory increases in our habitation, then the darkness is exposed to the light. The doors which had once shut in the tree of the knowledge of good and evil, is no longer shut but opened up by Holy Spirit, as He removes the reproach and shame that the enemy brought with that tree.

The Structure of Light cannot be comprehended by darkness; darkness loses! *"And the Light shines on in the darkness, for the darkness has never overpowered it [put it out or absorbed it or appropriated it, and is unreceptive to it]." John 1:5 Amp* "Light" here in Greek is *chrusŏs* and it means gold.[xxxi] The word *chrusŏs* derives from a root word in Greek *chraŏmai*, which means, "To furnish what is needed, give an oracle, to graze, employ, act toward one in a given manner, and entreat."[xxxii] This "gold" is the gold we can see Jesus depicting in Revelation 3:18, where He counsels us to buy "gold" refined in the fire. It takes the fire and trying of the Word of God to shine forth the Light!

Therefore, this gold (light) is the exchange of His Word that visits our soul and furnishes us with His power to fill our house. God's Word is employed in our person with power, to graze (touch) us in a given manner that manifest! (See 1 Corinthians 2:5).

When I minister in the prophetic by Holy Spirit and get in the Rivers of Living Water, Holy Spirit comes forth with the Light of Christ Jesus to touch people with the Word in Power, which restructures their soul, dismantling darkness and bringing forth the Light of God's Word. The Holy City is built up on the Light of truth, which is in the conscience (soul). The Kingdom of Heaven is brought near in these times, to set the captive free and bring the breath and life of God.

"I have come as a LIGHT INTO THE WORLD, so that whoever believes in Me [whoever cleaves to and trusts in and relies on Me] may not continue to live in darkness." John 12:46 Amp

"For God Who said, Let light shine out of darkness, has shone in our hearts so as [to beam forth] the LIGHT FOR THE ILLUMINATION of the knowledge of the majesty and glory of God [as it is manifest in the Person and is revealed] in the face of Jesus Christ (the Messiah)." 2 Corinthians 4:6 Amp

It is the structure of God's Light (The Word) that forever changes us. God clearly brings the light to shine in the darkness. This depiction of how Holy Spirit moves into our soul with the Light of Christ Jesus is depicted well in Genesis.

The Form of the Earth and the Form of Man

"1 IN THE beginning God (prepared, formed, fashioned, and) created the heavens and the earth. 2 The earth was without form and an empty waste, and darkness was upon the face of the very great deep. The Spirit of God was moving (hovering, brooding) over the face of the waters. 3 And God said, Let there be light; and there was light. 4 And God saw that the light was good (suitable, pleasant) and He approved it; and God separated the light from the darkness. 5 And God called the light Day, and the darkness He called Night. And there was evening and there was morning, one day." Genesis 1:5 Amp

Here in Genesis we see God in the beginning and how He prepared, formed and fashioned the heavens and the earth. Man came from the earth; God formed and fashioned man out of the ground of the earth. Therefore, the same substance in which God formed the earth was also the same substance in which God formed man. In looking at Genesis 1 we can receive a revelation.

Man became a "living soul" when God breathed into him and gave him life (Genesis 2:7). Something happened not only when God "formed" man but also once God breathed the breath of life into man. Likewise, before God fashioned the earth it was without form and it was empty waste; darkness was upon the face of the great deep, awaiting Holy Spirit (Breath) of God.

Did you know the human body is made up of 75 – 80% water when we are born, and it decreases a little over time as we age? Moreover, the human brain is composed of 85% water. Our human brain is made up of about 1,000,000 neurons! Those neurons have hundreds of trillion neuron groupings within them. Our neurons (brain cells) get together to form thoughts, which lead to the actions we carry out.

Water is a perfect conductor for electricity to flow in our brain. This makes it understandable, with all the different neuron groupings in our brain constantly at work, allowing a place of reception of power. This power in our brain actually looks like a light bulb and occurs from all the neurons firing off and communicating, which we will get into further in book 4 of "God's Fire Wall School of the Prophets – The Spirit of Knowledge."

Likewise, God showed me that the water in the brain could be compared to the water of the very great deep of Genesis 1. Therefore, the water in us, is likened unto the great deep of the earth, and in Genesis 1, it says "very great deep." Moreover, God showed me a long time ago that the word "earth" actually becomes "heart," when you move the "H."

"H" for us represents God's Holiness. When God's Holiness through Holy Spirit comes to us, we are no longer of the world "earth," but rather we are from above, the very "heart" of God. The word "deep" here in Genesis 1 means the subterranean water parts. The root word, from which it comes, is the Hebrew Word *hûwm* that means, "to make an uproar- move, make, noise."[xxxiii]

There was a deep place within the earth in Genesis 1, to which God spoke. When God spoke to the deep place, it caused movement, a stirring, which responded to the power of the spoken Word. Before there was light in the earth there was darkness upon the face of the very great deep, which was the place God spoke and caused movement.

The Lord showed me that this is likened to our soul, which is composed of the heart and mind (brain), which houses our will and emotions. As a man thinks in his heart so is he. (See Proverbs 23:7). Therefore, it is not thinking simply in our brain where the neuron groupings get together and give us thoughts, but it is how we think in our heart! The Power of God's Word reaches into our mind and heart to bring us the Word of Truth.

In Genesis 1, the "Spirit of God" moved across and brooded over the FACE OF THE WATERS. When God spoke over the waters "Let there be Light" it manifested, and came into being. God's Word caused movement in the very deep place, which was beneath the face of the waters. This movement brought about a roar, and a stirring, connecting the light into the DEEP.

The word "brood and hover" here in Hebrew is *râchaph* and means, "to brood, to be relaxed, to flutter, move, shake."[xxxiv] Brood means to hover over and protect according to Webster's Collegiate Dictionary. Hover means to "stay suspended or flutter in the air near one place; to linger or wait close by in overprotection, insistent."[xxxv] Therefore, God's Spirit was lingering, waiting close in a position of protection over what He formed and He spoke, which was "Let there be Light" and the light manifested! The Word manifested! Where God's Spirit is brooding, it is waiting for the Word of God so that a movement can be made toward manifesting the Word of God in the earth.

We are likened to the water in Genesis 1; we are likened to the earth without form, and where there was darkness upon the very great deep. The very great deep is our soul; the summation of who we are suited in our flesh. As God's Spirit hovered over the "FACE OF THE WATERS" it is likened to the presence of God hovering over us, brooding over us.

When His Word is spoken, it comes forth and goes to the very deep, of our soul, stirring our spirit man up and causing our soul to move towards the Word, and it brings forth the light of Christ Jesus. The Word is made known to our soul giving us a renewed spiritual mind.

Likewise, what we see in the visible is true of what is going on in the "invisible." This spiritual mind, by the working and power of God's Word, is being transformed.

Our body is merely a capsule for our soul and spirit. Our face, which is indicative in Genesis 1 as God brooding over the "FACE" of the very great deep, displays what is inside of us. The light in us doesn't come from our body, but rather the light of Jesus comes from our soul (the great deep) and is resident on our face, which is known as our "countenance."

Therefore, the more we are healed in our soul, the more increased measure of the light of Christ Jesus will be seen on our face! We have the treasure of Jesus in us! It is literally Christ in us the Hope of glory that is seen on display! We see this truth displayed in the face of Christ.

"6 FOR GOD, WHO SAID, "LET LIGHT SHINE OUT OF DARKNESS, "MADE HIS LIGHT SHINE IN OUR HEARTS TO GIVE US THE LIGHT OF THE KNOWLEDGE OF GOD'S GLORY DISPLAYED IN THE FACE OF CHRIST. 7 BUT WE HAVE THIS TREASURE IN JARS OF CLAY TO SHOW THAT THIS ALL-SURPASSING POWER IS FROM GOD AND NOT FROM US." 2 Corinthians 4:6-7 Amp

When God said let there be light, he divided the darkness from the light and said it is good and called the darkness night and the light day. In our soul, there are places of darkness that need the Light of Christ Jesus in order to bring forth a transformation of our spiritual mind so we think in our heart according to what God's Word says about us.

The Word becomes "Day" to us! Although God spoke the Word while hovering over the 'face of the waters' it went to the "very great deep of the water" where there could be movement. It is when the engrafted word gets into our soul, to the deep places that it brings the light of Christ Jesus! That is why it is important to get the Word of God in the deep places.

I have so many people saying "Robin you are too deep," but it is because of this depth that I walk where I am in the Light of God's glory! Moreover, the work of the enemy against my soul was in the "deep place," and because it was God had to go to that depth to set me free! He whom is forgiven much loves much! (See Luke 7:47) I was forgiven in the depths of my soul that had been in the prison and here God was releasing me from it!!! I was like the woman who had the Alabaster bottle and that bottle was my soul, given for the display and infilling of God's Glory! (My spiritual daughter, Theresa Chapel Harbin drew this picture of me at Jesus' feet as the woman with the Alabaster bottle.)

The "very great deep" can be seen in our soul, even through science.

"The central theses of cardio-energetics, that the heart and not the brain is where our most basic thoughts, feelings, fears, and dreams are gently but profoundly mediated."

"Neurotransmitters found in the brain have also been identified in the heart, establishing a direct neurochemical and electrochemical communicational link between the heart and the brain beyond the purely neurological connections known to exist between the brain and the heart."

"The heart, through hormones, neurotransmitters, and what scientists call subtle quantum energies, exerts at least as much control over the brain as the brain exerts over the heart."

"Drs. John and Beatrice Lacey of the National Institute of Mental Health report that there is direct evidence that the heart neurohormonally calls for a constant environmental update from the brain in order to organize the energy of the body."[xxxvi]

Do you see this? There is an energy that comes as a result of the connection between our brain and heart. The evidence reveals this occurs because of the thought processes that are not occurring in the brain, but rather the ones that take place in the heart. As the heart has thoughts in it as well, it has a constant update not only from the brain but also to the brain! Therefore, as our spirit man (in our belly) stirs by Holy Spirit, it in turn stirs up the Word of God that is in our heart, yielding a standing grain harvest, which brings about the renewed and transformed mind!

This all comes from the connection between our heart and our brain. The neurons in the brain come together and release the light of the Word of truth. When neurons come together and communicate ,it is through neuron synapses, which we will get more into in book 4 of God's Fire Wall School of the Prophets – The Spirit of Knowledge. I do not want to get too much into this science today but rather lay out the fact that our brain and heart update continually, creating quantum type energy that can be picked up by scientists.

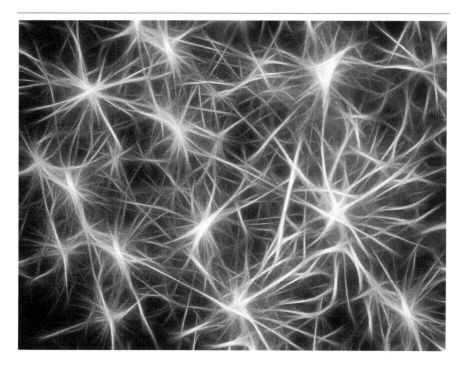

The communications of synapses when firing look like that of a light bulb. It is through the axon of the brain cell, that causes a release through the axon terminals, across the synapses to reach other brain cells that we see what is called, "synapses firing." When you see "synapses firing" it reveals the light that occurs in our mind. Literally "there is light," as in Genesis 1. Communications in the brain that groups neurons together and releases thoughts into our mind, which communicate with the heart, have this constant light process occurring.

It is in the heart that belief is determined. From what our heart believes we then are able to see the soul of a person.

Therefore, as God's Word says He has written His law upon our hearts, it is in our heart that we think and believe. Our soul is seen in our heart and mind. The inner working of the relationship and inner connectedness of the heart and brain, show the STRUCTURE of LIGHT that is being established in our soul by the Word of God.

As we think in our heart (our soul) so are we! When we have places in our soul that need healing, it is because that place of our soul does not line up with the word of God. Instead the enemy has a hook in our emotions, manipulating our soul, as he feeds us from the tree of the knowledge of good and evil, binding us in fear and shame. Thus, it is necessary for us to eat God's Word, to bring the Light of Christ Jesus; it is this light that pierces our soul and overcomes all darkness.

"4 In Him was Life, and the Life was the Light of men. 5 And the Light shines on in the darkness, for the darkness has never overpowered it [put it out or absorbed it or appropriated it, and is unreceptive to it]." John 1:4-5 Amp

That is what happened to my soul; God pierced the dark places of my soul to bring the light and life of Jesus Christ! When I married my first husband that abuse brought a lot of darkness into my soul, where the lies of the enemy pulled me into bondage. I conveniently shut the door on the darkness and did not want to deal with it; I didn't have the power to overcome it. However, after I was confronted with the truth of the darkness that was in my life, I could no longer avoid it because it tormented my soul.

All I longed for was freedom, where the enemy could no longer torment my soul. I wanted more of Jesus in me! Blessed are those that are hungry and thirsty for righteousness for they shall be filled! (See Matthew 5:6) Holy Spirit was brooding over my soul (heart and mind), stirring my spirit, going into the very deep places within my soul that would cause uproar, a movement within my soul, WHERE DEEP WOULD CALL UNTO DEEP!

"7 [Roaring] deep calls to [roaring] deep at the thunder of Your waterspouts; all Your breakers and Your rolling waves have gone over me." Psalm 42:7 Amp

The depths of God's soul, His Spirit, called unto my soul and spirit and began to bring a movement of hunger and thirst of righteousness that I had not known before. It was the increased hunger and thirst for Jesus' righteousness that caused God to respond to my soul by bringing the revealing of His Word that had been hidden in my heart!!! In the place of my heart that hungered, God brought revelation by Holy Spirit to a depth of my spirit that communicated to my heart the very thoughts of God!!

As I began to walk in the mind of Christ Jesus I found the thoughts of my heart transforming my mind, where I began to go from glory to glory in the knowledge of God's Glory! I began to gaze and behold His glory as if I was staring in a mirror with an unveiled face, and as a beheld His glory; I was being transformed into that likeness! The very Glory of God is His mind and opinions that hold the weighty matters of eternity. This very same mind reveals to us our value in the Light of His Word.

God filled me with His Life breathed Word and continued to speak to my soul the light of truth, separating the light from the darkness. As I continued in faith reading God's Word, it accelerated me in the holiness of Who He is, causing me to be that garden that is shut up and is a fountain with streams from Lebanon!!!!! The streams from my heart, the breath of God that flows out and speaks to my mind, gives my soul peace and causes me to know Him more.

"But you are a chosen race, a royal priesthood, a dedicated nation, [God's] own purchased, special people, that you may set forth the wonderful deeds and display the virtues and perfections of Him Who called you out of darkness into His marvelous light." 1 Peter 2:9 Amp

"The people who walked in darkness have seen a great Light; those who dwelt in the land of intense darkness and the shadow of death, upon them has the Light shined." Isaiah 9:2 Amp

It is where eternity is locked up in our hearts that the light of Christ Jesus shines, the Law of God's Word, which is written and unlocked by Holy Spirit bringing us into Truth, so we walk in the ancient paths, the eternal paths, out of darkness and into God's light.

"16 And I will bring the blind by a way that they know not; I WILL LEAD THEM IN PATHS THAT THEY HAVE NOT KNOWN. I will MAKE DARKNESS INTO LIGHT BEFORE THEM AND MAKE UNEVEN PLACES INTO A PLAIN. THESE THINGS I HAVE DETERMINED TO DO [FOR THEM]; AND I WILL NOT LEAVE THEM FORSAKEN". Isaiah 42:16 Amp

Chapter 6 Bronze Gates and Iron Bars

The bondage we are in when we find ourselves in darkness looks like bronze gates and iron bars. We see this clearly depicted in Psalm 107 and in Isaiah 45:1-3

"Thus says the Lord to His anointed, to Cyrus, whose right hand I have held to subdue nations before him, and I will unarm and ungird the loins of kings to open doors before him, SO THAT GATES WILL NOT BE SHUT. 2 I WILL GO BEFORE YOU AND LEVEL THE MOUNTAINS [TO MAKE THE CROOKED PLACES STRAIGHT]; I WILL BREAK IN PIECES THE DOORS OF BRONZE AND CUT ASUNDER THE BARS OF IRON. 3 AND I WILL GIVE YOU THE TREASURES OF DARKNESS AND HIDDEN RICHES OF SECRET PLACES, THAT YOU MAY KNOW THAT IT IS I, THE LORD, THE GOD OF ISRAEL, WHO CALLS YOU BY YOUR NAME." Isaiah 45:1-3 Amp'

"16 FOR HE HAS BROKEN THE GATES OF BRONZE AND CUT THE BARS OF IRON APART. 17 Some are fools [made ill] because of the way of their transgressions and are afflicted because of their iniquities. 18 They loathe every kind of food, and they draw near to the gates of death. 19 Then they cry to the Lord in their trouble, and He delivers them out of their distresses. 20 HE SENDS FORTH HIS WORD AND HEALS

THEM AND RESCUES THEM FROM THE PIT AND DESTRUCTION. 21 Oh, that men would praise [and confess to] the Lord for His goodness and loving-kindness and His wonderful works to the children of men! 22 And let them sacrifice the sacrifices of thanksgiving and rehearse His deeds with shouts of joy and singing! 23 Some go down to the sea and travel over it in ships to do business in great waters; 24 These see the works of the Lord and His wonders in the deep. 25 For He commands and raises up the stormy wind, which lifts up the waves of the sea. 26 [Those aboard] mount up to the heavens, they go down again to the deeps; their courage melts away because of their plight. ... ...33 He turns rivers into a wilderness, water springs into a thirsty ground, 34 A fruitful land into a barren, salt waste, because of the wickedness of those who dwell in it. 35 He turns a wilderness into a pool of water and a dry ground into water springs; 36 And there He makes the hungry to dwell, that they may prepare a city for habitation, 37 And sow fields, and plant vineyards which yield fruits of increase. 38 He blesses them also, so that they are multiplied greatly, and allows not their cattle to decrease. 39 When they are diminished and bowed down through oppression, trouble, and sorrow, 40 He pours contempt upon princes and causes them to wander in waste places where there is no road. 41 Yet He raises the poor and needy from affliction and makes their families like a flock. 42 THE UPRIGHT SHALL SEE IT AND BE GLAD, BUT ALL INIQUITY SHALL SHUT ITS MOUTH. 43 Whoso is wise [if there be any truly wise] will observe and heed these things; and they will diligently consider the mercy and loving-kindness of the Lord. Psalm 107:16-26, 33-43 Amp

History records that there were 100 gates of bronze in Babylon. By setting up iron bars they were able to close these huge bronze doors, and keep them from opening. The security of the bronze doors and Iron bars ensured that it would be impossible for anyone to come into and defeat Babylon.

Moreover, the wall was 86 feet thick and 344 feet high. The wall was so thick, that chariot races use to be held on top of the wall. Here God prophesies about Cyrus who will go into Babylon (a place that took Israel captive) and get the treasures of darkness. Moreover, we see the words that God will make every crooked place straight and bring down every mountain, inferring the preparation for the Lord.

History records that when Cyrus went into Babylon to retrieve the treasures they had stolen from nations, including Israel, the doors were wide open, and the hardest thing he had to do was to load the treasure and move it! God opened the doors that had been shut and brought Cyrus in as the Light of His Word to set the captive free!

We see in Psalm 107:16 the psalmist declares, *"for He has broken the gates of bronze and cut the bars of iron."* This breaking of the gates of bronze represents the places we could not get through into victory. The bars of iron represent the enemy's stronghold on our lives. In this place God sends His Word to rescue us from this pit! *"He sends forth His Word and heals them and rescues them from the pit of destruction." Psalm 107:20 Amp* As God sends His Word it causes us to be glad, knowing that he is causing iniquity's mouth (satan our adversary) to be shut, removing the reproach of sin and shame off us. *"But all iniquity shall shut its mouth"* (indicating the removal of sin nature out of our soul). This is what happens when the light of truth comes! It pierces the hardest walls, penetrating into our heart, where our heart swells up and is glad by the anointing that destroys the yoke of bondage!

All through Section 1 of Structure in this book "The Light" you have seen the distinction between darkness and light. In addition, we see the analogy of God likening us to "a garden" where we see the tree of the knowledge of good and evil and the Tree of Life. Moreover, God compares our soul to the great deep of the earth in Genesis 1, where we see the stirring of man's soul by Holy Spirit to cause the Word of God to enter the thoughts of our heart and renew our mind. Finally, we see the darkness of the enemy that keeps us bound up is like a castle that has thick walls and doors, as well as bars of iron. The revealing of all of these complexities in God's Word shows the inner relationship of the issues of our soul.

Chapter 7 A City on A Hill

"14 YOU ARE THE LIGHT OF THE WORLD. A CITY SET ON A HILL CANNOT BE HIDDEN." Matthew 5:14 Amp

As we looked in the first section, "Structure," we saw the Structure of the Light of God's Word, which is in us. Here in Matthew 5:14 Jesus declares our structure; The Light, Jesus is our structure! He compares the structure of Light we are while in this world, likened to that of a "CITY" set on a hill. Therefore, as we look at our soul, it can be compared to a city on a hill. In this paradigm it begins to shift us to see from the perspective of the condition of our soul and more from the viewpoint of heaven, through the eyes of God. The enemy would cause us to put a flogger to our soul and condemn it because that is what satan brought, condemnation. However, Jesus is the opposite and He does not condemn us but relieves us from condemnation by saving us.

"1 THEREFORE, [there is] now no condemnation (no adjudging guilty of wrong) for those who are in Christ Jesus, who live [and] walk not after the dictates of the flesh, but after the dictates of the Spirit. 2 For the law of the Spirit of life [which is] in Christ Jesus [the law of our new being] has freed me from the law of sin and of death. 3 For God has done

what the Law could not do, [its power] being weakened by the flesh [the entire nature of man without the Holy Spirit]. Sending His own Son in the guise of sinful flesh and as an offering for sin, [God] condemned sin in the flesh [subdued, overcame, deprived it of its power over all who accept that sacrifice], 4 So that the righteous and just requirement of the Law might be fully met in us who live and move not in the ways of the flesh but in the ways of the Spirit [our lives governed not by the standards and according to the dictates of the flesh, but controlled by the Holy Spirit]." Romans 8:1-4 Amp

We are in Christ Jesus, our New Life, which is where we are freed from the law of the curse of sin and death. Our spirit is born from above when we have Jesus Christ as our Lord and Savior. For those people that are not saved yet, for whom you are praying, this is where the Ephesians 1:17-19 prayer comes in, because it is only the light of Christ Jesus coming to a soul by Holy Spirit that brings the plan of salvation.

God showed me years ago that the spirit of ungodly religion comes to people and says, "you are saved" although it is a lie and not truth, the person truly believes that they are saved. However because it was not the Spirit of Truth that spoke to them, they are not saved. That is why people can be going to church and still go to hell; they think they are saved but it is only God that saves us and offers us salvation! The fruit of the person is evidence as to whether or not they are walking in the salvation of Christ Jesus. (See Matthew 12:33) It does not mean we are perfect when we are saved, but we are seeking God and are being perfected. That is why I love the Ephesians 1:17-19 prayer. When you pray this, you are praying that Holy Spirit brood over the soul of that person to speak to their soul and bring forth THE LIGHT!

"17 [For I always pray to] the God of our Lord Jesus Christ, the Father of glory, that He may grant you a spirit of wisdom and revelation [of insight into mysteries and secrets] in the [deep and intimate] knowledge of Him, 18 By having the eyes of your heart flooded with light, so that you can know and understand the hope to which He has called you, and how rich is His glorious inheritance in the saints (His set-apart ones), 19 And [so that you can know and understand] what is the immeasurable and unlimited and surpassing greatness of His power in and for us who believe, as demonstrated in the working of His mighty strength," Ephesians 1:17-19 Amp

This particular scripture calls forth God's Spirit of Wisdom, the Spirit of Knowledge and Spirit of Understanding by Holy Spirit that work cooperatively together in bringing a person forth into the plan of salvation and it is all by God's Spirit! Therefore, if someone is not saved this is the prayer you would pray in the healing of their soul so they can begin the process of letting the light of Christ Jesus shine in their soul to bring healing, pulling them out of darkness and into God's marvelous light so they eat of the Tree of Life.

THE CITY!

The revelation in God's Word is that we are a light that cannot be hidden, a city on a hill. God took me through His word and showed me the revelation of how our soul is likened to a city. He began giving me more understanding and revelation of why Nehemiah wept over the desolation of the city Jerusalem. As Holy Spirit took me to the book of Nehemiah He than began showing me man's soul before salvation. Our soul is like the desolate city of Jerusalem in the book of Nehemiah. Our soul is in ruins, and is desolate requiring the work of God by Holy Spirit who consoles us to bring forth complete healing through salvation.

As I began to study the Nehemiah 1, Holy Spirit unveiled revelation to God's structure of what our soul looks like when we come to Him and how the healing process continues until we are made whole. The teaching I did in 2011 "Awake, Awake Oh Sleeper the Warrior Bride is a Holy City," opened my eyes to how Holy Spirit works through me when I minister to someone. So many people time after time have spoken to me how they received breakthroughs, healings and deliverances in their soul as never before, after a time of ministry.

Holy Spirit opened my eyes to the scripture of the Holy City and showed me how the Holy City is within a soul of a believer. We have to see that Holy City in order to speak truth and build it up (repair and renovate the soul) with the power of God's Spirit.

The enemy can cause us to be so bound up in areas of our soul that a person's true personality is not seen. God created every person and gave us our personality for the Call of God on our lives. As we grow into spiritual maturity, more of our personality comes forth from where it has been hidden. Its as the psalmist says that we have been in a narrow place, asking for God to bring us into the broad place.

"7 I will be glad and rejoice in Your mercy and steadfast love, because You have seen my affliction, You have taken note of my life's distresses, 8 And You have not given me into the hand of the enemy; You have set my feet in a broad place. 9 Have mercy and be gracious unto me, O Lord, for I am in trouble; with grief my eye is weakened, also my inner self and my body." Psalm 31:7-9 Amp

This is what it is like when you are working in the healing process of the soul with another person. When the person is stuck in a dark place, that is the "narrow place," and causes their soul trouble. Holy Spirit in you helps build up the Holy City and speak Life and Light to them, so they can come out of that narrow place. This process in reality is Isaiah 45:1-3 the breaking down of bronze doors and iron bars that have held people captive to bring them, as a treasure out of darkness, out into God's marvelous light.

To begin healing of the soul we have to see what our soul is too look like in the fullness of God's healing. It is to look like the Holy City in Revelation 21.

"1 THEN I saw a new sky (heaven) and a new earth, for the FORMER SKY AND THE FORMER EARTH HAD PASSED AWAY (VANISHED), AND THERE NO LONGER EXISTED ANY SEA. 2 And I saw the holy city, the NEW JERUSALEM, DESCENDING OUT OF HEAVEN FROM GOD, ALL ARRAYED LIKE A BRIDE BEAUTIFIED AND ADORNED FOR HER HUSBAND, 3 Then I heard a mighty voice from the throne and I perceived its distinct words, saying, SEE! THE ABODE OF GOD IS WITH MEN, AND HE WILL LIVE (ENCAMP, TENT) AMONG THEM; AND THEY SHALL BE HIS PEOPLE, AND GOD SHALL PERSONALLY BE WITH THEM AND BE THEIR GOD. 4 God will wipe away every tear from their eyes; and death shall be no more, neither shall there be anguish (sorrow and mourning) nor grief nor pain any more, for the old conditions and the former order of things have passed away. 5 AND HE WHO IS SEATED ON THE THRONE SAID, SEE! I MAKE ALL THINGS NEW. Also He said, Record this, for these sayings are faithful (accurate, incorruptible, and trustworthy) and true (genuine). 6 AND HE [FURTHER] SAID TO ME, IT IS DONE! I AM THE ALPHA AND THE OMEGA, THE BEGINNING AND THE END. TO THE THIRSTY I [MYSELF] WILL GIVE WATER WITHOUT

PRICE FROM THE FOUNTAIN (SPRINGS) OF THE WATER OF LIFE. 7 HE WHO IS VICTORIOUS SHALL INHERIT ALL THESE THINGS, AND I WILL BE GOD TO HIM AND HE SHALL BE MY SON. Revelation 21:1-7 Amp

Here we see the Holy city no longer has any of the old; the old earth and old sea are vanished. We will reach this position fully when we go to be with the Lord in glory; however, we are to reach maturity in the soul before we ever leave this life. What we do, what we learn, what we implement in this lifetime affects our rewards in eternity.

It is essential for us to yield to Holy Spirit in order that God can bring healing in our soul, taking us from one dimension of glory to another dimension of glory in His Word. We can only enter a dimension of glory (God's Copiousness) for which our soul has been prepared. God knows how much we can bear and will not put on us more than we can bear. This not only relates to trials and tribulations, but also relates to how much of God's glory we can bear.

As God prepared Moses to see His glory, He also prepares us to see His glory by transforming our mind into the mind of Christ Jesus. (See 1 Corinthians 2:16) In the glorified soul, resembled in Revelation 21, the old structures and mindsets of the carnal man vanish. There is no more pain and sorrow, no more tears. The soul that is glorified has no more wounds, which could stir up pain, sorrow or grief; God makes all things new!

We are to be victorious in our lifetime in pursuing God's Word, which will bring renewal to our spiritual mind, as He brings us comfort in this earth until that glorious day we go home to be with Him. This process of the soul is to work out our salvation in fear and in trembling, so we do not partake in the depravity of the fallen nature through the tree of the knowledge of good and evil.

"8 But as for the cowards and the ignoble and the contemptible and the cravenly lacking in courage and the cowardly submissive, and as for the unbelieving and faithless, and as for the depraved and defiled with abominations, and as for murderers and the lewd and adulterous and the practicers of magic arts and the idolaters (those who give supreme devotion to anyone or anything other than God) and all liars (those who knowingly convey untruth by word or deed)--[all of these shall have] their part in the lake that blazes with fire and brimstone. This is the second death." Revelation 21:8 Amp

The Word of God clearly describes the open doors to a person's soul, which would allow the enemy a right to torment us. The list includes but is not limited to unbelief, being faithless, depraved and having defiled abominations, being a murderer, adulterous, idolater, practicing magic arts, etc. Holy Spirit gives us revelation that if we have any of these evil practices that we do not inherit the Kingdom of God. In reading this we have to understand that grace raises the standard where murder is now speaking hatefully against another.

Therefore, we are to repent from evil and yield ourselves to the Lordship of Christ Jesus, allowing Holy Spirit to work out any tares the enemy sowed in our soul that might be a result of this mindset. Moreover, since the curse passes down even three generations, you might have inherited this from someone in your family. It is necessary to allow Holy Spirit to show you areas in which you are being attacked in your soul even from generational sin committed against God by our ancestors, so we can repent and allow the door to be shut to that place in our soul. Once you repent of these areas, by faith trust that God will work out the performance of His Word.

"9 Then one of the seven angels who had the seven bowls filled with the seven final plagues (afflictions, calamities) came and spoke to me. He said, Come with me! I will show you the bride, the Lamb's wife 10 Then in the Spirit He conveyed me away to a vast and lofty mountain and exhibited to me THE HOLY (HALLOWED, CONSECRATED) CITY OF JERUSALEM DESCENDING OUT OF HEAVEN FROM GOD, 11 Clothed in God's glory [in all its splendor and radiance]. The luster of it resembled a rare and most precious jewel, like jasper, shining clear as crystal. 12 It had a massive and high wall with twelve [large] gates, and at the gates [there were stationed] twelve angels, and [on the gates] the names of the twelve tribes of the sons of Israel were written ... ... 22 I SAW NO TEMPLE IN THE CITY, FOR THE LORD GOD OMNIPOTENT [HIMSELF] AND THE LAMB [HIMSELF] ARE ITS TEMPLE. 23 AND THE CITY HAS NO NEED OF THE SUN NOR OF THE MOON TO GIVE LIGHT TO IT, FOR THE SPLENDOR AND RADIANCE (GLORY) OF GOD ILLUMINATE IT, AND THE LAMB IS ITS LAMP. 24 The nations shall walk by its light and the rulers and leaders of the earth shall bring into it their glory. 25 And its gates shall never be closed by day, and there shall be no night there. 26 They shall bring the glory (the splendor and majesty) and the honor of the nations into it. 27 But nothing that defiles or profanes or is unwashed shall ever enter it, nor anyone who commits abominations (unclean, detestable, morally repugnant things) or practices falsehood, but only those whose names are recorded in the Lamb's Book of Life." Revelation 21:9-27

The Holy City Jerusalem as it is in heaven, is the prototype of what a whole soul looks like. There is a splendor and radiance inside of the soul, where that soul has become a habitation for God. There is no need for a light for the Lord God's temple, because God and the Lamb are the Light of the Temple for the Holy City.

As we come into salvation by God's Holy Spirit revealing to us that Jesus is the Christ, the Son of God, Who came to earth as Son of God and Son of Man, died for our sins, and was resurrected, the Holy City within us takes root, it starts to shine. While I minister, Holy Spirit gives me visions to see the Holy City within the person that is growing, the Light of Christ Jesus. As I see the Holy City within someone, God will have me speak life to "build up" the Word of God, through the "Spirit of Prophecy." The Spirit of Prophecy is distinguished from the gift of prophecy and I go into this in the book "God's Fire Wall School of the Prophets Session 1 Elohim." The anointing of the spirit of prophecy breaks yokes of oppression and causes the person to arise and shine.

As God instructed Jeremiah,

"9 Then the LORD reached out his hand and touched my mouth and said to me, "I have put my words in your mouth. 10 See, today I appoint you over nations and kingdoms to uproot and tear down, to destroy and overthrow, to build and to plant." Jeremiah 1:9 Amp

Likewise, we uproot and tear down lies of the enemy in the souls of others, by the leading and prompting of Holy Spirit. We only do what Holy Spirit gives us the "green light" to do. I have learned by God's Holy Spirit that He will tell you when to bind and when to deliver someone from a devil attacking their soul. In order for that person to get set free and delivered, the Holy City within them has to increase so that they can "walk in that freedom."

If the person is not ready for deliverance, and we try to do deliverance in our own strength, the devil will try and harm and tear the soul. Therefore, you do NOTHING until God shows you what to do, when you minister to someone else. That is why it is good to take God's Fire Wall School of the Prophets along with Healing of the Soul.

In circumstances where the Holy City is not built up enough according to what God is showing me, then I can only bind the devils from operating against that soul. However, when Holy Spirit gives me the green light to command that devil to leave a person it is because the Word, Jesus, is built up in them. When Jesus Christ is built up in a person then the anointing in them swells up and snaps the yoke of oppression. This is why it is so important to tell people to read the Word of God. If the person is not there yet you can pray Ephesians 1:17-20 and ask that Holy Spirit give them an increase hunger and thirst for righteousness.

When we are ministering to a person's soul and we have uprooted the lies of the enemy and have torn down demonic strongholds at Holy Spirit's prompting, we then build up the Holy City within the vessel by the Word of God, as Holy Spirit leads us. The engrafted Word of God is the means by which you build up the Holy City, declaring it to the person through scripture.

God always tears down, destroys and uproots the attacks of the enemy, before He builds and plants His Word. Holy Spirit showed me that many times when I minister to most people (not all but most) there needs to be some uprooting, tearing down and destroying of the enemy's lies before God can release the prophetic Word to build up.

The image Holy Spirit gave me was the parable of the sower of seed in Mark 4. Some seed was sown on thorny ground and did not take root, because of the cares of this world choking it out. Some fell on stony ground but it did not have deep roots during the time of the persecution of the Word.

The good ground (soil) that seed fell on, harvested some 30, some 60 and some 100 fold. When we minister to a soul with the Spirit of Prophecy, and the seed of the Word is sown on thorny or stony ground, our efforts are fruitless. Therefore, the healing of the soul assists in removing those thorns, plowing that ground of the soul in order that the seed of God's Word can take deep root and bear 30, 60 or 100 fold.

When you look at the Holy City Jerusalem you see 12 gates and at each gate an Angel of the Lord is stationed. It is no different with our soul. We are to have the Lord enthroned in our soul, guarding us and keeping us from evil.

Chapter 8 The Place Where God's Name Dwells

As I stated earlier, the wounded soul looks desolate and is depicted as the city Jerusalem, which Nehemiah the prophet wept over. It is in this book of God's Word that Holy Spirit unveils our soul and its desolation briefly in chapter 1 and goes into further detail in Chapter 2. Here we will look at chapter 1 of Nehemiah and go deeper in the next sessions to the different structures of the city Jerusalem.

"1 THE WORDS or story of Nehemiah son of Hacaliah: Now in the month of Chislev in the twentieth year [of the Persian king], as I was in the castle of Shushan, 2 Hanani, one of my kinsmen, came with certain men from Judah, and I asked them about the surviving Jews who had escaped exile, and about Jerusalem. 3 And they said to me, The remnant there in the province who escaped exile are in great trouble and reproach; the wall of Jerusalem is broken down, and its [fortified] gates are destroyed by fire. 4 When I heard this, I sat down and wept and mourned for days and fasted and prayed [constantly] before the God of heaven, 5 And I said, O Lord God of heaven, the great and terrible God, Who keeps covenant, loving-kindness, and mercy for those who love Him and keep His commandments, 6 Let Your ear now be attentive and Your eyes open to listen to the prayer of Your servant which I pray before You day and night for the Israelites, Your servants, confessing the sins of the Israelites which we have sinned against You. Yes, I and my father's house have sinned

. 7 We have acted very corruptly against You and have not kept the commandments, statutes, and ordinances which You commanded Your servant Moses. 8 Remember [earnestly] what You commanded Your servant Moses: If you transgress and are unfaithful, I will scatter you abroad among the nations; 9 But if you return to Me and keep My commandments and do them, though your outcasts were in the farthest part of the heavens [the expanse of outer space], YET WILL I GATHER THEM FROM THERE AND WILL BRING THEM TO THE PLACE IN WHICH I HAVE CHOSEN TO SET MY NAME. 10 Now these are Your servants and Your people, whom You have redeemed by Your great power and by Your strong hand. 11 O Lord, let Your ear be attentive to the prayer of Your servant and the prayer of Your servants who delight to revere and fear Your name (Your nature and attributes); and prosper, I pray You, Your servant this day and grant him mercy in the sight of this man. For I was cupbearer to the king." Nehemiah 1:1-11 Amp

When I worked in the mental health arena-counseling clients with all sorts of mental health diagnosis it was evident that their souls were disarrayed and fragmented. Likewise when I went through the abuse I endured with my first marriage, my soul became tormented and torn by the enemy. It is understandable to see how science somehow depicts the reason in which a person's soul has different personalities due to abuse by hypothesizing about the souls fragmentation. When abuse is so intense that if the person were to actually live through the event, some part of their soul would have to fragment, because of having the knowledge of this evil act committed against them. Therefore, when I looked at this scripture, Holy Spirit revealed to me a deeper meaning in order to understand the process of the wounded soul.

At first we see the book of Nehemiah start with an introduction of names. *"1THE WORDS or story of Nehemiah son of Hacaliah: Now in the month of Chislev in the twentieth year [of the Persian king], as I was in the castle of Shushan, 2 Hanani, one of my kinsmen, came with certain men from Judah, and I asked them about the surviving Jews who had escaped exile, and about Jerusalem." Nehemiah 1:12 Amp* Nehemiah is introduced, and then his identification is linked to his father's name. The name Nehemiah means "consolation" and is made of two Hebrew words, *nâcham* meaning, "to console" and *Yâhh* meaning "the sacred name of the Lord most vehement."[xxxvii] The two Hebrew names link up to give us a picture of a God that is Jealous, because His Name is Jealous and is stirred up vehemently to console us! This revelation of God as the "Consoler," the Comforter is depicted in the attributes of Holy Spirit. *"26 But when the COMFORTER (Counselor, Helper, Advocate, Intercessor, Strengthener, Standby) comes, Whom I will send to you from the Father, the Spirit of Truth Who comes (proceeds) from the Father, He [Himself] will testify regarding Me." John 15:26 Amp*

Holy Spirit is our Comforter! God by His Spirit brings forth vehemently His plans and purposes making us whole as delineated in Isaiah 9:7. *" Of the INCREASE OF HIS GOVERNMENT AND OF PEACE there shall be no end, upon the throne of David and over his kingdom, to establish it and to uphold it with justice and with righteousness from the [latter] time forth, even forevermore. The ZEAL OF THE LORD OF HOSTS WILL PERFORM THIS." Isaiah 9:7 Amp*

God brings His government, His Word, His rule and increases peace, which in Hebrew means restitution, being made whole, complete and restoration. God brings Heaven to Earth in us! The Kingdom of Heaven comes near as a result of God building us up. Therefore, we see "Nehemiah" the name, is revelation of Holy Spirit Who comes to our soul and brings the New Structure.

The month in Nehemiah 1:1 is Chislev, and is the time in which Jews celebrate Hanukkah, also known as the Festival of Lights! The Festival of Lights is for the lighting of the Menorah in the Temple in the Holy Place. Again, the Holy Place represents Holy Spirit inside of our soul, as well as our soul within, which is in relationship to God because our spirit is now born from above. As Holy Spirit is inside of us He brings forth the truth of God's light in our spirit man that is then stirred up by Holy Spirit, causing our soul to hunger and thirst for the light of truth. Our soul is waiting in the Holy of Holies for the infilling of that Glory brought forth by Holy Spirit to show us the Father through God's Word.

Moreover, Nehemiah 1:1 takes place, while Nehemiah was in the castle of the King of Persia, of Shushan. Shushan actually means "lily" in Hebrew. As we look at a lily here, it also gives us revelation in the book of Nehemiah, comparing it to the Shulammite who is like a lily in the valley surrounded by thorns.

"2 But Solomon replied, Like the lily among thorns, so are you, my love, among the daughters." Song of Solomon 2:2 Amp

The thorns represent the trials of the lily in a place of darkness as the enemy of her soul is buffeting her, but it is here where she grows, according to Song of Solomon 2:1. In this time of trying and testing, God is bringing forth the time of feasting and celebrating of the Light!

Nehemiah is the son of Hacaliah as stated in verse 1. *Hacaliah* in Hebrew means "darkness of Jah."[xxxviii] Does that not blow your mind; it is even in God's Word that He is with you in your darkness! What is interesting is the word Haclaiah not only means "darkness of Jah," but it also means "Illumination!" It is when you are in the darkness that you get the ILLUMINATION THAT WAS SENT INTO THE WORLD! Therefore, the Healing of the Soul of man is not "the dark night of the soul," but rather "THE GREAT LIGHT OF THE SOUL!"

He is both God of the light and God of the darkness as we see in Genesis 1, when He separated the darkness from the light. We are not talking about evil here. What we are distinguishing in this verse is not the darkness of evil, but in the darkness God brings illumination (Gods' Word- Jesus) to our soul. Jesus is the Pure Light sent from above to illumine every man. (See John 1:9)

Before anything came into being over the earth there was great darkness. God sees the darkness and brings forth "THE LIGHT!" In the book of Nehemiah, God is speaking that Holy Spirit will come forth and bring comfort to the places in our soul where there is darkness. Those areas in which we have struggled with darkness (wrestling) are simply waiting for the revealing of Christ Jesus. As God shines His light in the midst of the darkness of our soul, veils are removed from our face, in order for that we behold His glory. It is this glory, that we are transformed into the likeness of Christ.

"18 And all of us, as with unveiled face, [because we] continued to behold [in the Word of God] as in a mirror the glory of the Lord, are constantly being transfigured into His very own image in ever increasing splendor and from one degree of glory to another; [for this comes] from the Lord [Who is] the Spirit." 2 Corinthians 3:18 Amp

In the Tabernacle as depicted earlier, there is the outer court, the inner court (Holy Place), and the Holy of Holies. Although there is illumination and light in the Holy Place by the menorah being lit, indicating Holy Spirit, there is still the Holy of Holies that is kept behind heavy curtains. The curtains are so thick that there is complete darkness behind the curtains and only the Light of God is what illuminates the Holy of Holies. God is God of the Holy of Holies!

Your soul is the Holy of Holies, which God fills with His Light! Before God enters the Holy of Holies there is utter darkness! God is God of the darkness as well as the Light, because He separates the light from the darkness. Before we see the light of God break forth in our souls we have to contend when Holy Spirit tells us to, by waiting upon the Lord until the Light comes forth. This is not depression or sadness, but rather it is where we confront places in our soul that need the illumination of God in order to bring wholeness and healing. We see this indicated when we suffer fiery trials and tribulations that is the testing of our faith (belief in our heart). These trials are our darkness, causing us to wait on God. They are allowed in order to show us the "Word" so that we wait in faith for that Word to come to that place in our soul that has been in bondage.

For example, when I was in bondage to alcoholism, everything in me tried to medicate and deliver myself from that bondage. No matter what I did, I could not set myself free. It was when God told me to use the Word of His truth and me getting to the end of myself, knowing that I could not set myself free, that finally His visitation of Light came to my soul, entering that chamber of darkness to shine the light of truth!!!!! In that moment the light pierced my soul, causing more light to fill me, so my eye would continue to fulfill its office and take the light of truth to all areas of my soul.

One of Nehemiah's kinsmen, Hanani, comes to him with men from Judah, and gives Nehemiah the news about the condition of Jerusalem. *Hanani* means "gracious" and *Judah* means "praise and celebrated." Therefore, as we see the grace of God come by the power of Holy Spirit, it brings praise in our soul where God can be celebrated. This praise is from God alone and not anything we can do in your own strength; it is God praising Himself through us!

God is gracious and it is through the garment of praise that the cloak of heaviness is lifted off our soul. (See Isaiah 61:3). *Jerusalem* means "God has founded peace." Therefore, the destiny and pronouncement of the city Jerusalem is to be heaven on earth; as it is in heaven it is on earth. When Nehemiah hears from Hanani that Jerusalem is broken down and the fortified gates destroyed by fire, he is given God's strength to see what Hanani has seen. God gives Nehemiah the grace to see through God's eyes so he can have God's heart for Jerusalem. Nehemiah begins to weep and mourn for days, praying and fasting. The condition of Jerusalem has so touched Nehemiah's heart that he is restless to see the city restored!

Likewise, Holy Spirit is restless to see us restored in our soul. It grieves Holy Spirit that we are in a saddened state of oppression from the enemy. He is vigilant and violent in performing the Word that God sends Him to manifest. As Nehemiah grieves here, we see how God's heart grieves for the restoration and reconciliation of His children.

Nehemiah begins to first remind God about His covenant and His Name. God made covenant with Israel through Abraham, but God's Name was shown to Moses. Therefore, Nehemiah reminds God of both His covenant and His Name (His nature). Then Nehemiah does something unique; he does not separate himself from the Israelites; he identified with their sins, claiming, "We have sinned." The humanity of Nehemiah in ministering to God's people reveals that he seeks a right heart with the Lord and knows that he is not too proud to repent of that which he does not even know. This is true humility, as we see Christ Jesus is without sin, He took on sin and nailed it to the cross. The identification Nehemiah reveals, allows us to see that we have a High Priest, Who without sin is able to empathize with our frailty. (See Hebrews 4:12-16)

When we minister in the area of the Healing of the Soul we maintain a position of humility knowing that like Paul, we are chief sinner. It is only by God's grace, that we are able to do anything. Hanani represents God's grace to Nehemiah because Nehemiah humbled himself. Nehemiah gives attention to God's covenant that was broken, acknowledging God, and the result of sin (from iniquity), causing God to scatter His people abroad and among the nations.

Likewise there are two areas in which our soul is in darkness. One area is simply because we have not had the light of Christ Jesus come to that area of our soul, but again that changes because of salvation. Another way, we see here in Nehemiah is because of sin that has separated us from God. Those areas in our soul that have the sin nature and is in darkness has been shut up and waiting on the healing light of Christ Jesus to enter, piercing us with the light of His truth. Our soul that has the sin nature in it is compartmentalized away from the part that does have the Light of Jesus. It is a veil as indicated in 2 Corinthians 3:18 that needs to be removed. God longs to fellowship with us, and the greater our healing the greater the fellowship. He removes veils from our face by the Spirit of the Lord so that we walk in liberty.

God's word promises as Nehemiah reminded God, that *"if you return to Me and keep My commandments and do them, though your outcasts were in the fartherest part of the heavens [the expanse of outerspace], yet will I gather them from there and will bring them to the place in which I have chosen to set My Name." Nehemiah 1:9 Amp* Here is where God revealed to me how the soul becomes fragmented and disassociates. Because we have knowledge of the tree of good and evil in our person, this itself is the transgression of the law. It has been committed upon our person, and as a result our soul seems at times fragmented.

God is gracious and causes our soul to be in a place where He separates the light from the darkness, which is what we see in Nehemiah 1:8-9. We see this war that Paul describes with the carnal nature at work in our members in Romans 7. Paul says he does what he doesn't want to do and doesn't do what he wants to do, and if it is no longer him doing it then it is that sin principle at work in his members. (See Romans 7:18-19) This sin principle operates in the soul, and it is this place that God brings the light of His truth.

God's Word promises that as we seek God and obey Him, that the parts of our soul that are fragmented and torn apart, separated by the sin nature from the Light of Christ Jesus that God would indeed gather those parts of our soul and bring them to the place where He has chosen to "set" His Name! Set here in Hebrew is *shakan* pronounced *shä·kan'* meaning "lodging, reside permanently, abide, continue, dwell, habitation, inhabit, remain, rest and set up."[xxxix]

Looking at the Hebrew letters that compose this word "set," gives us deeper understanding. I will not give too much until we move further into year 3 of God's Fire Wall School of the Prophets, but I want to provide a few words when Holy Spirit leads me. The Hebrew letters that compose the word "set" are Sheen, Kaph and Nun. The ancient symbol for the Hebrew letter "Sheen" is teeth and also indicates fire, meaning, "to consume" in the positive and "to devour" in the negative. The Hebrew letter Kaph is the ancient symbol of the palm of a hand and means, "covering, open and allow." Finally, the ancient symbol for the Hebrew letter "Nun" is a fish swimming through water and it means "activity and life." Therefore, the word picture you have for the Hebrew word "set," is **THE CONSUMING FIRE THAT COVERS YOU AND BRINGS LIFE!!!!**

ASSIGNMENTS

In praying for your soul this month ask God to expose to the light the desolate places within you that have been torn down and destroyed by the enemy; the enemy comes to steal, kill and destroy but Jesus comes to bring life and life abundantly. (See John 10:10) In those places begin to call forth Joel 2:25-29.

In ministering to others begin to call forth Ephesians 1:17-19.

Chapter 9 Illumination

Here in the class ILLUMINATION we combine the "STRUCTURE" and the "REVELATION," by asking GOD to bring "ILLUMINATION OF THE WORD" This part of the School of Healing of the Soul by combining "Structure" and "Revelation," is a greater understanding of the Word. One thing Holy Spirit taught me is to point people to God, to Holy Spirit, to Jesus. Holy Spirit tells us all things and only speaks what the Father is speaking, which always testifies of Jesus. Therefore, ask Holy Spirit to cause you to see God's Word.

The following is a revelation of how a desolate city looks like but by the Light of Christ Jesus is made whole. God is a God that gives to us more than we could ever think or imagine according to His power in us that is in operation. (See Ephesians 3:20) God is always increasing His power in us by Holy Spirit so that His Word is operative in greater authority. That is why we go from glory to glory and authority to authority, as our soul is healed; we have more of the presence of Christ Jesus in us!

"1 SING, O barren one, you who did not bear; break forth into singing and cry aloud, you who did not travail with child! For the [spiritual] children of the desolate one will be more than the children of the married wife, says the Lord. 2 Enlarge the place of your tent, and let the curtains of your habitations be stretched out; spare not; lengthen your cords and strengthen your stakes, 3 For you will spread abroad to the right hand and to the left; and your offspring will possess the nations and make the desolate cities to be inhabited. 4 Fear not, for you shall not be ashamed; neither be confounded and depressed, for you shall not be put to shame. For you shall forget the shame of your youth, and you shall not [seriously] remember the reproach of your widowhood any more." Isaiah 54:1-4 Amp

God shows us in Isaiah 54 how the process of barrenness in our soul, causes us to cry out for His presence. The barren woman for this session represents the areas in which we have experienced tribulations of our soul where we are aware of the darkness, from which we need freedom. We have knowledge of the sin that is present and operating within our members and we feel that the reproach will never be removed. It is in this area that we know of the darkness we are sitting in and we are waiting for the Light of Christ Jesus.

Here the barren woman is told to stretch her tent pegs. The reason that she is stretching her tent pegs is that there is more room for God's presence to dwell. We are looking at the barren woman's "curtains" which are indicative of the "curtain" to the Holy of Holies! This means that the soul is about to be filled with the LIGHT! As a result, she is able to see the increase of light take over. This light of the Lord God removes the reproach of her widowhood, which represents feeling forsaken because of that sin nature at operation in her members.

As we get freedom, knowing there is nothing good in us except Christ Jesus, then God brings forth His power, as He reveals His presence, causing us to know that our Maker is our Husband, He is our COVERING! He covers our shame; His love covers a multitude of sins! It is here where we are enveloped by God's love that is divinely expressed in the healing and deliverance He brings the soul.

The barren woman's offspring (indicating the Word of God within her) will now go and possess the desolate places. These desolate places represent the attacks of the enemy against our soul. As God's Word multiplies in our soul, it brings down the nations and kingdoms that have exalted themselves against the Name of Jesus; that is where God brings all of the fragments of our soul, to the place where His Name dwells!

"5 For your Maker is your Husband--the Lord of hosts is His name--and the Holy One of Israel is your Redeemer; the God of the whole earth He is called. 6 For the Lord has called you like a woman forsaken, grieved in spirit, and heartsore--even a wife [wooed and won] in youth, when she is [later] refused and scorned, says your God. 7 For a brief moment I forsook you, but with great compassion and mercy I will gather you [to Me] again. 8 In a little burst of wrath I hid My face from you for a moment, but with age-enduring love and kindness I will have compassion and mercy on you, says the Lord, your Redeemer. 9 For this is like the days of Noah to Me; as I swore that the waters of Noah should no more go over the earth, so have I sworn that I will not be angry with you or rebuke you. 10 For though the mountains should depart and the hills be shaken or removed, yet My love and kindness shall not depart from you, nor shall My covenant of peace and completeness be removed, says the Lord, Who has compassion on you." Isaiah 54:5-10 Amp

Here we see as our Maker is the Lord of Hosts, this is the Name He uses for battle. In this Name He battles on our behalf in His righteousness to bring down the adversary of our soul, who is satan! God comes as redeemer, redeeming us from the curse that has been a reproach and a stronghold. We see Him saying that He forsook the barren woman briefly but this is not God forsaking us; He will never leave us or forsake us. Remember this is all from the barren woman's perspective and to her it feels as though her darkness separated her from God. On the contrary He says, as it was in the days of Noah, that His promise would be firm as He lifted up the banner of His covenant over her.

As the barren woman goes through this shaking she sees that the Covenant of God has not weakened in her own soul but rather she finds it amazingly strengthened! Though everything depart and be shaken God assures His covenant is firmly established with the Isaiah 54 barren woman. Is it not interesting that the Hebrew word for "set" looks and sounds much like our English word for "shaken?" She has gone through a shaking and has come out established by God on the other side of this trial being "set."

"11 O you afflicted [city], storm-tossed and not comforted, behold, I will set your stones in fair colors [in antimony to enhance their brilliance] and lay your foundations with sapphires. 12 And I will make your windows and pinnacles of [sparkling] agates or rubies, and your gates of [shining] carbuncles, and all your walls [of your enclosures] of precious stones. 13 And all your [spiritual] children shall be disciples [taught by the Lord and obedient to His will], and great shall be the peace and undisturbed composure of your children 14 You shall establish yourself in righteousness (rightness, in conformity with God's will and order): you shall be far from even the thought of oppression or destruction, for you shall not fear, and from terror, for it shall not come near you." Isaiah 54:11-14 Amp

God's Word reveals the afflictions of the barren woman's trial, which seems a horrific storm, where she lacked comfort. However, in the midst of the storm God was with her. In this place, God speaks of the beauty of her brilliance, which is represented by jewels, but these jewels are symbolic of revelations of the Life of God's Word. At the depiction of the beauty of the Isaiah 54 woman's holiness, we see that the Lord will teach her spiritual offspring. Here the offspring represents those whom the Word of the Lord is taught; God is the teacher of the spiritual offspring, who are disciples of God.

God taught the barren woman how to hear His voice in the darkness and in that place she knows the still small voice of God that gives strength and directs! She now teaches others the Word of Truth that causes enlargement of God's Kingdom.

Her establishment is one thing, THE RIGHTEOUSNESS OF CHRIST JESUS! In this righteousness all of hell trembles because it is this righteousness that is a coat of mail against the gates of hell, causing them to be pushed back. The Life and Light of God's Word is so large in the Isaiah 54 woman that she is firmly established as a standard of righteousness, sending the enemy fleeing.

"15 Behold, they may gather together and stir up strife, but it is not from Me. Whoever stirs up strife against you shall fall and surrender to you. 16 Behold, I have created the smith who blows on the fire of coals and who produces a weapon for its purpose; and I have created the devastator to destroy. 17 But no weapon that is formed against you shall prosper, and every tongue that shall rise against you in judgment you shall show to be in the wrong. This [peace, righteousness, security, triumph over opposition] is the heritage of the servants of the Lord [those in whom the ideal Servant of the Lord is reproduced]; this is the righteousness or the vindication which they obtain from Me [this is that which I impart to them as their justification], says the Lord." Isaiah 54:15-17 Amp

In this place of victory, the adversary has no power. He cannot stir up strife in the soul of the Isaiah 54 woman because the battle she has won has instead increased the light of truth. The power of this place has brought the barren woman into victory and now she has become a weapon of mass destruction against the powers of darkness! The very thing that warred against her soul is the very thing she has authority to destroy. No tongue of the adversary that would come against her would be able to prosper, because her identity is in the Name of the Lord and not herself. His Name is set up large in her tent and He dwells in the midst of that habitation!

Likewise, as you are delivered and set free in your soul, you will go, grow and glow from GLORY TO GLORY! You will rise up in greater authority and power, knowing the Word of God as never before, as you overcome by the Blood of the Lamb and the Word of your testimony! (See Revelation 12:11)

Therefore, take Isaiah 54 and identify the following

Assignments

Declare these scriptures over you by speaking them and meditate on these scriptures in your mind throughout the day. John 1:5; Jeremiah 29:11-13; Isaiah 9:7; Ephesians 1:17-20 & Ephesians 3:16-21

Have you noticed places in which you feel like the barren woman, forsaken? Look at examples as it relates to interactions with others or circumstances.

What lies of the enemy has attacked your soul, that you by God's Word are bringing the truth, to show it wrong?

Declare Isaiah 54 over you this month.

---

[i] "Swaddle." Oxford University Press. *The Oxford American College Dictionary*. Published G.P. Putnam's Sons, 2002

[ii] "Envelop." Oxford University Press. *The Oxford American College Dictionary*. Published G.P. Putnam's Sons, 2002

[iii] "Structure." Oxford University Press. *The Oxford American College Dictionary*. Published G.P. Putnam's Sons, 2002.

[iv] James Strong, *Strong's Expanded Exhaustive Concordance of The Bible*, (Nashville, Thomas Nelson, 1990) Strong's Concordance Hebrew word # 6108 "substance"

[v] James Strong, *Strong's Expanded Exhaustive Concordance of The Bible*, (Nashville, Thomas Nelson, 1990) Strong's Concordance Hebrew word # 6105 "make strong"

[vi] James Strong, *Strong's Expanded Exhaustive Concordance of The Bible*, (Nashville, Thomas Nelson, 1990) Strong's Concordance Hebrew word # 6106 "life"

[vii] James Strong, *Strong's Expanded Exhaustive Concordance of The Bible*, (Nashville, Thomas Nelson, 1990) Strong's Concordance Hebrew word # 6763 "rib"

[viii] James Strong, *Strong's Expanded Exhaustive Concordance of The*

Bible, (Nashville, Thomas Nelson, 1990) Strong's Concordance Hebrew word # 1129 "build"

[ix] "Complex." Oxford University Press. *The Oxford American College Dictionary*. Published G.P. Putnam's Sons, 2002

[x] James Strong, *Strong's Expanded Exhaustive Concordance of The Bible*, (Nashville, Thomas Nelson, 1990) Strong's Concordance Hebrew word # 6725 "Zion"

[xi] James Strong, *Strong's Expanded Exhaustive Concordance of The Bible*, (Nashville, Thomas Nelson, 1990) Strong's Concordance Greek word # 5460 "illumination"

[xii] James Strong, *Strong's Expanded Exhaustive Concordance of The Bible*, (Nashville, Thomas Nelson, 1990) Strong's Concordance Greek word # 3788 "eye"

[xiii] James Strong, *Strong's Expanded Exhaustive Concordance of The Bible*, (Nashville, Thomas Nelson, 1990) Strong's Concordance Greek word # 3700 "gaze"

[xiv] James Strong, *Strong's Expanded Exhaustive Concordance of The Bible*, (Nashville, Thomas Nelson, 1990) Strong's Concordance Greek word # 3088 "lamp"

[xv] James Strong, *Strong's Expanded Exhaustive Concordance of The Bible*, (Nashville, Thomas Nelson, 1990) Strong's Concordance Hebrew word # 5647 "tend and guard"

[xvi] James Strong, *Strong's Expanded Exhaustive Concordance of The Bible*, (Nashville, Thomas Nelson, 1990) Strong's Concordance Hebrew word # 5315 "soul"

[xvii] James Strong, *Strong's Expanded Exhaustive Concordance of The Bible*, (Nashville, Thomas Nelson, 1990) Strong's Concordance Hebrew word # 7302 "watered"

[xviii] James Strong, *Strong's Expanded Exhaustive Concordance of The Bible*, (Nashville, Thomas Nelson, 1990) Strong's Concordance Hebrew word # 7301 "to water"

[xix] James Strong, *Strong's Expanded Exhaustive Concordance of The Bible*, (Nashville, Thomas Nelson, 1990) Strong's Concordance Hebrew word # 3844 "Lebanon"

[xx] James Strong, *Strong's Expanded Exhaustive Concordance of The Bible*, (Nashville, Thomas Nelson, 1990) Strong's Concordance Hebrew word # 3825 "heart"

[xxi] James Strong, *Strong's Expanded Exhaustive Concordance of The Bible*, (Nashville, Thomas Nelson, 1990) Strong's Concordance Hebrew word # 7725 "restore"

[xxii] James Strong, *Strong's Expanded Exhaustive Concordance of The Bible*, (Nashville, Thomas Nelson, 1990) Strong's Concordance Greek word # 3056 "word"

[xxiii] James Strong, *Strong's Expanded Exhaustive Concordance of The Bible*, (Nashville, Thomas Nelson, 1990) Strong's Concordance Greek word # 3004 "to lay forth"

[xxiv] James Strong, *Strong's Expanded Exhaustive Concordance of The Bible*, (Nashville, Thomas Nelson, 1990) Strong's Concordance Greek word # 225 "truth"

[xxv] James Strong, *Strong's Expanded Exhaustive Concordance of The Bible*, (Nashville, Thomas Nelson, 1990) Strong's Concordance Greek word # 2990 "unawares"

[xxvi] James Strong, *Strong's Expanded Exhaustive Concordance of The Bible*, (Nashville, Thomas Nelson, 1990) Strong's Concordance Greek word # 2222 "life"

[xxvii] James Strong, *Strong's Expanded Exhaustive Concordance of The Bible*, (Nashville, Thomas Nelson, 1990) Strong's Concordance Hebrew word # 5903 "naked"

[xxviii] James Strong, *Strong's Expanded Exhaustive Concordance of The Bible*, (Nashville, Thomas Nelson, 1990) Strong's Concordance Hebrew word # 6174 "naked"

[xxix] James Strong, *Strong's Expanded Exhaustive Concordance of The Bible*, (Nashville, Thomas Nelson, 1990) Strong's Concordance Greek word # 3339 "transform"

[xxx] James Strong, *Strong's Expanded Exhaustive Concordance of The Bible*, (Nashville, Thomas Nelson, 1990) Strong's Concordance Greek word # 342 "renewing"

[xxxi] James Strong, *Strong's Expanded Exhaustive Concordance of The Bible*, (Nashville, Thomas Nelson, 1990) Strong's Concordance Greek word #5557 "light."

[xxxii] James Strong, *Strong's Expanded Exhaustive Concordance of The Bible*, (Nashville, Thomas Nelson, 1990) Strong's Concordance Greek word #5530. "employ"

[xxxiii] James Strong, *Strong's Expanded Exhaustive Concordance of The Bible*, (Nashville, Thomas Nelson, 1990) Strong's Concordance Hebrew word #1949. "deep"

[xxxiv] James Strong, *Strong's Expanded Exhaustive Concordance of The Bible*, (Nashville, Thomas Nelson, 1990) Strong's Concordance Hebrew word #7363 "brood"

[xxxv] Webster's New World Dictionary 2nd Collegiate Edition pg. 681

[xxxvi] Pearsall, Paul PhD, The Heart's Code, Broadway Books, NY pg. 68

xxxvii James Strong, *Strong's Expanded Exhaustive Concordance of The Bible*, (Nashville, Thomas Nelson, 1990) Strong's Concordance Hebrew word #5162 "Nehemiah"

xxxviii James Strong, *Strong's Expanded Exhaustive Concordance of The Bible*, (Nashville, Thomas Nelson, 1990) Strong's Concordance Hebrew word # 2446 "Hacaliah"

xxxix James Strong, *Strong's Expanded Exhaustive Concordance of The Bible*, (Nashville, Thomas Nelson, 1990) Strong's Concordance Hebrew word # 7931 "set"

Made in the USA
San Bernardino, CA
20 January 2019